Colleges, Learning and Libraries: the Future

Also in this series

Conflict and change in library organizations
by Ken Jones

The information professions in the electronic age
by John Gurnsey

LOOKING FORWARD IN LIBRARIANSHIP

Colleges, Learning and Libraries: the Future

Peter J. Pack and F. Marian Pack

Series editor: Alan Day MA MPhil PhD DipLib FRGS FLA
Head, Department of Library and Information Studies,
Manchester Polytechnic

CLIVE BINGLEY  LONDON

© F. Marian Pack and Peter J. Pack 1988

Published by
Clive Bingley Limited
7 Ridgmount Street
London WC1E 7AE

First published 1988

British Library Cataloguing in Publication Data
Pack, Peter J.
    Colleges, learning and libraries : the future. — (Looking forward in librarianship).
    1. Great Britain. Further education institutions. Libraries
I. Title   II. Pack, F. Marian   III. Series 027.7'0941

    ISBN 0-85157-397-5

Typeset in 10/12pt Times by Style Photosetting Ltd,
Tunbridge Wells, Kent.
Printed and made in Great Britain by Redwood Burn Ltd,
Trowbridge, Wiltshire.

Contents

Acknowledgements

We would like to acknowledge the assistance of many librarians and other learning resource professionals when writing this book. Situated in rural Cumbria we have experienced 'distance writing' (as opposed to distance learning) at first hand! Our former colleges, Edge Hill and Salford, have been generous in the loan of books and reports and we have drawn on the material and bibliographic resources of Lancaster University Library. The British Library, both the Document Supply Centre and the Library Association Library, has been another valuable resource.

Providing executive services for the Learning Resources Development Group has been a great benefit. Through it we have maintained an active participation in college learning resource matters. In particular, the articles in the *Learning Resources Journal* have been a major source of contemporary material.

We would like to express our thanks to all those whose advice and comments have, directly or indirectly, influenced the writing of this book. This includes the many publishers who have granted us permission to quote from their authors' works. Finally, the advice, support and patience of Library Association Publishing Ltd should not go unremarked.

Note: Personal pronouns present a problem. We have decided to use the masculine form 'he' and 'his' to cover both sexes when the need arises instead of a lengthier and clumsier alternative.

Introduction

What do we mean by a 'college'?

A word of qualification is required at the start since the term 'college' can cover institutions from sixth-form colleges to polytechnics and university colleges. It covers both advanced and non-advanced further education, frequently within a single institution. The authors are writing primarily about those colleges that are within their own experience. In one case this was teacher education and colleges of higher education; in the other, colleges of technology and further education.

Having said that, many of the issues that are discussed have wide application throughout further and higher education and readers should relate them to their own situation.

Finally, we have not tried to cover the Scottish education system or Scottish colleges, although, as we have just said, doubtless many of the issues will have equal relevance north of the border.

Who is this book for?

Among the groups which we believe will find the book of interest are:

1   *Students of librarianship:* although this is in no sense a student textbook there are some contexts in which the book could be useful. These are:

- Specialist courses on educational librarianship.
- During fieldwork placement in colleges. This would be particularly true for students who have no previous college library experience and need to absorb something of the background.
- In conjunction with studies and theses on college librarianship.

2   *Librarians who are new to colleges:*
- Students entering college library work – during their period of work experience leading to full qualification.
- Librarians moving into colleges from other types of library work.

3   *College librarians:* we see this book as fulfilling two main functions: an explanation of the college background and an expression of professional opinions against which they can measure and develop their own ideas.

ix

4 *Other resource professionals:* where the library operates in conjunction with other learning resource agencies with some pattern of coordination the book could provide a useful 'window' into the activities and attitudes of librarians for the educational technologist and the computer specialist.

5 *College management:* there may be members of senior management who assume overall responsibility for college resource provision. This book could provide a useful insight into one of the largest central organizations within this field.

6 *Other librarians:* this would be a useful addition to any librarianship collection for the use and staff development of librarians in other types of library.

What this book is about

Any book is a reflection of the author's knowledge, perceptions, understandings and opinions. This work is no exception, dealing with a specialized subject and attempting to discuss the relationship between a profession and its clients while at the same time analysing the complex interaction between two professions, education and librarianship, in the context of the college. It is not a textbook. In no sense does it compete with works like the Library Association's *College Librarianship*, which is one of a series of handbooks on library *practice*. It makes no claims to comprehensiveness; its treatment of library topics is selective.

We have tried to set the college library in its context. For this reason the book is divided into two parts, the first of which deals entirely with the educational situation. The historical survey is intended to give the librarian a background and a perspective to colleges. The second chapter identifies certain features which seemed to us sufficiently important to be dealt with in greater detail. The second element in the first part is management. The college is considered as a system and then its particular characteristics are examined. This is followed by a look at the effects of contraction and uncertainty on colleges. Part 1 ends with a chapter on educational technology and educational objectives. This is intended to be a bridge from the institutional background to the college library itself. The library must function in the context of the college, therefore the librarian must appreciate the educational needs and objectives of the institution.

At the start of Part 2, 'Aspects of the college library', we return to the systems approach. The library as a system parallels our earlier discussion of the college as a system, indeed the library is a subsystem of the college. It brings out two aspects of demand and influence upon the college library – student need and college requirement, something which was indentified in the consideration of teacher-centred courses and student-centred learning. The idea of a proactive library, responding to client needs, is developed.

The other chapters on aspects of the college library are:

- The topics which are most likely to be exercising the minds of college librarians at the present time.
- The issues which we believe will have an important bearing on the future.

The impact of information technology is of major significance. We need to consider its effect on the nature of learning, and the implications for more individualized and interactive approaches as well as the more obvious concerns of librarians about automating library operations. This has been couched in college terms, therefore we have concentrated on microcomputer-based applications. We make no apology for looking to the future and speculating about fifth-generation computing since we believe that this will have a fundamental impact on both further and higher education as well as revolutionizing the role of the library.

The other main topic is the changing pattern of resource organization. This can have a major effect on the library, coordinating it with other learning resource agencies. In the last chapter we consider the major resource in the library, the professional librarian, and raise questions of identity, relationships and staff development.

And finally . . .
We hope this is a book to make you think. While some parts may inform, we hope that we have never lapsed into 'information for information's sake'. The approaches, ideas and arguments are based on considerable experience and observation on both our parts.

To the librarian we would say: if it makes you consider, or reconsider (or even react to our views about) some activity or attitude towards your students, academic colleagues, management, other library staff, operations or performance, then we shall have succeeded.

To those who are not librarians but are reading this book to gain some insight into the college library and those who are responsible for it, we would hope that the impression you gain is positive but not aggressive, forward-looking yet grounded in understanding and common sense. Above all we hope the approach is cooperative and constructive, enabling, indeed requiring, librarians to play their part in developing the quality of learning in our colleges.

Part 1
SETTING THE CONTEXT

Chapter 1   The main developments in public sector higher and further education since 1970

This chapter is intended to give a perspective and to help to answer the questions 'Where are we now?' and 'How did we arrive here?'

Education is constantly changing since it responds to needs which are themselves constantly developing and modifying. As well as educational needs, changes are prompted by influences that are political, legal, social, economic and cultural.

The last two decades have been especially turbulent but there are two significantly different emphases in the nature of the changes. The penultimate decade was *expansionist,* the one through which we are presently passing is *reductionist.*

Expansion

During the period from 1948 to 1973 the number of students in full-time further and higher education had increased from 47,000 to 264,000 and part-time day students from 222,000 to 712,000. In 1948 there were 7,000 students on full-time, teacher-training courses whereas by 1972 the number was over 10,000 with another 1,400 given one-year, full-time release for advanced study.

In terms of gross national product, education expenditure increased from 2.8% to 6.6% of the total.

Quantitative growth offered opportunities at the same time for qualitative improvement. Increased overall expenditure with greater numbers of participants and a greater teaching force offered scope for more subject options and curricula that could be more diverse. During this period of expansion there was also an attitudinal change with a greater appreciation of the value of educational quality in promoting economic growth – the human/capital theory and the establishment of the view that a better educated workforce would provide more adaptable, innovative and productive workers. Education on a broader base would produce people capable of developing management skills, creativity, entrepreneurial expertise which in turn would provide the supportive infrastructure needed in the move

3

to more service-orientated industries and away from manufacturing which was the trend beginning to dominate in the economy during this period.

After the Second World War education was in a favourable situation – it thrived in a climate of economic growth aided by increased demand and had many spokesmen to back it. Spending on defence initially declined; social services and other national departments had not yet begun to make demands or gained sufficient political support.

The spate of reports and White Papers of the 1950s and 1960s are evidence of the ferment of interest and the positive approach. This was the era of Crowther[1] and Robbins.[2] Command Papers appeared on the growth in technical education,[3] opportunities in technical education,[4] industrial training,[5] polytechnics[6] and the Open University.[7]

Ministry and later Department of Education committees reported on general studies in technical colleges,[8] day release[9] and technical teacher training[10] – in all cases highlighting the need for greater provision.

All this activity on paper was followed up by approval of major building programmes, improvement in salary scales and conditions of service for teachers and an increase in the number of sandwich and block-release courses.

The year 1964 saw the establishment of the Council for National and Academic Awards (CNAA) – a development from the National Council for Technological Awards – and with it the advent of degree course provision by institutions other than the universities, thus generating a large increase in opportunity for qualification to degree level and significantly in specifically vocationally-orientated areas of study.

Contraction

The downturn period was presaged in print in a 1972 Command Paper ironically entitled *Education: a framework for expansion*.[11] This White Paper forecast that the previous ten years of major educational expansion would go on for at least another ten years and the intention was expressed that the education service should continue to contribute fully to the vitality of both society and the economy.

Almost immediately this expectation was voiced, however, the situation began to show signs of change. Industrial problems began to manifest themselves on the home front and these were greatly exacerbated by the quadrupling of oil prices as a result of the

4

Arab–Israeli war. This began a change in the world economic climate which is still reverberating and many of whose manifestations are still readily apparent.

By 1980 an expected rate of expansion of 4% in real terms had been replaced by the prospect of negative growth of the same proportions.

Government measures to counter the declining economic situation and its consequences soon began to appear – some with 'general' application, e.g. the introduction of cash limits and ratecapping, (which nevertheless quickly affect the labour-intensive education service), and others quite specifically related to education, e.g. DES circular 2/74[12] detailing spending restrictions service by service, the capping of the advanced further education pool, the debate relating to student funding and the Audit Commission exercise.

Economic decline, inflation, effects of high levels of public expenditure, higher tax levels with their impediments on industrial developments and the ensuing rampant unemployment levels had a twofold effect on the educational scene, particularly the further and higher sector:

- Contraction/expansion factors
- Unemployment problem initiatives

Contraction/expansion factors
Demographic and economic predictions would lead one to expect a continued contraction in demand in the education system though it cannot be absolutely assumed that the actual contractions already taking place in the compulsory sector will be mirrored in the post-compulsory scene. There are arguments both for and against. It is not easy to predict whether the proportion of school leavers taking up post-compulsory education will increase – the social bias in the birth rate decline might suggest this. The effects of unemployment could affect the take-up in either direction. Potential students could argue that improved qualifications enhance their job prospects or even simply that they might as well be occupied in some worthwhile pursuits to fill their increased leisure time. Some, on the other hand, will argue the futility of becoming more qualified when prospects of employment seem so remote.

The 'bird in the hand' philosophy might encourage some to take jobs with fewer development prospects at the first opportunity rather than taking time to qualify further and enhance their own potential. Yet again decreases in student funding, deferment of eventual higher salaries, possible income foregone and the quality and availability of courses – assuming contraction in provision as another factor of economic retrenchment – may affect study take-up adversely.

Political issues such as 'the 21 hour rule' which limited study by unemployed 16 to 19-year olds to less than 21 hours per week if they wished to claim supplementary benefit, the lure of the training allowances built into the MSC scheme, the disparity of course funding when colleges undertake MSC-sponsored schemes side by side with existing 'similar' courses all have an influence on the balance of work and enrolments.

Comments made at the November 1985 CBI Conference in Harrogate, where speakers urged that education should be treated as a priority area of investment, show an interesting shift of emphasis:

> Any further cuts in higher education will starve industry of graduate talent and endanger the economy. . . . It was time businessmen stopped blaming teachers for industry's unfavourable image and set about selling themselves purposefully to schools.
>
> *(TES,* 22 Nov., 1985).[13]

Further CBI comments in reply to the Green Paper on Higher Education would indicate industrial support for the higher and further education sector, but this support must be earned:

> The decline (i.e. in demand) is unlikely to be as large as that projected in the Green Paper. Indeed it is to be hoped that some part of the drop in numbers of 18-year-olds seeking places will be offset by increasing numbers of mature students seeking updating and upgrading of qualifications in mid-career. Current policy and successive reductions in funding have seriously undermined morale and effectiveness in HE establishments. The 1986 White Paper on HE should seize the opportunity to repair the damage. In return for a commitment to level funding through to 1995 government should require a commitment from HE to pursue vigorously internal reforms and reorganization, to accept changes to the infrastructure under which it operates.
>
> *(NATFHE Journal,* Feb. 1986).[14]

At the time of writing, CBI reactions to the White Paper (Cm 114)[15] have not appeared in the media. A complex structure is proposed for funding and the transfer via contracts from one sector to another but it is not obvious what commitments will be made to funding – though the Government Public Expenditure White Paper[16] makes it quite clear that additional expenditure will be minimal. What is certain, though the Education White Paper says manpower planning is impracticable, is the greater emphasis that colleges will be obliged to give to accountability, rationalization and linkage with industry.

This has become a major issue in the mind of the Secretary of State for Education. The poor performance of the education and training system compared with those of the country's competitors, in providing a workforce that is competent to meet the changing needs of industry and to meet the 'new' challenges of information/computer technology are documented variously in a spate of government and government-related publications viz: *Competence and competition,* NEDO;[17] *Skills shortages report,* MSC;[18] *Employment, the challenge for the nation,* Cmnd.9474;[19] *Review of vocational qualifications;*[20] *Training for Jobs,* Cmnd.9135;[21] *The development of higher education into the 1990s,* Cmnd.9524;[22] *Higher education: meeting the challenge,* Cm 114.

At the instigation of RSA and with support from government, CBI, TUC and other major industrial, professional and educational institutions, 1986 was designated 'Industry Year'.[23] Its aim was to 'encourage a better understanding of industry its essential role and its service to the community and to win acceptance for it'.

The latest government initiative with this emphasis, at the time of writing, is the Open College. Announced in July 1986 by Lord Young, Secretary of State for Employment, the first year of recruitment began in September 1987. Initial take-up was smaller than anticipated, the cost and initial range of courses proving a limiting factor. The aim of the Open College is to use open learning to widen access to training in an extensive range of skills, up to degree level. Courses are designed to help students improve their occupational competence. The expectation is that such improvement will ultimately have a favourable effect upon economic performance in the United Kingdom.

Colleges are under pressure to provide substantial changes in the type and range of courses offered, suggesting considerably expanding needs in some areas with a plethora of accompanying resource problems in terms, for example, of expensive investment programmes for equipment updating and staff development and retraining programmes in a climate of reduced funding. This expansion and redevelopment has to be set against rapid decline in some of the more traditional course areas. All this has been and is being undertaken in a climate of very real contraction in the form of staff establishment cuts and reorganizations, initially in some instances due to the merging of several institutions and latterly in the pursuit of voluntary redundancy and early retirement programmes. Real fears are being expressed about redundancy implications of the 1987 White Paper.

More worrying for NATFHE is the hint that new negotiating arrangements for FE lecturers will be set up once the White Paper becomes law.
As employers, polytechnics and colleges will be expected to reach 'local
agreements' with staff. But, warns the consultative paper, they should not
take on board the 'no redundancy' deal struck between many authorities
and the lecturers' union. NATFHE fears that this 'far from reassuring
statement' could herald large-scale redundancies.

(Education, 17.4.87).[24]

Outcomes from these developments have highlighted the need for
concentration of thought by college planners on issues that may have
been allowed to drift in the earlier, more lax days of relative plenty.
Certain official prompts have come the way of colleges via the
deliberations of such bodies as the NAB, the Audit Commission, the
Lindop Committee, CNAA, CATE, and the 1987 HMI Report, as
well as being spelled out in some detail in the 1987 White Paper (Cm
114). The need to examine, rationalize and justify provision of
courses; to evaluate, assess and consider in cost-effective terms the
need for more systematic collection and use of college management
data to assist efficiency and effectiveness (e.g. FEMIS); the need in
some instances to make choices between Advanced and Non-Advanced Further Education; or indeed the need to protect non-
advanced courses in the light of new funding policies instigated by the
NAB – all these and more are issues being earnestly debated in the
harsh economic climate of today.

Indeed, it has recently become clear that the NAB itself is to go out
of existence and divisions between the sectors will be more marked
and reorganization of funding policies make financing yet more
complex.

These are proposed outcomes of *Higher education: meeting the
challenge*[25] which spells out the government's intentions to 'secure
the re-establishment of the polytechnics and other institutions of
substantial size engaged predominantly in higher education as
free-standing outside local authority control'. Substantial size means
over 350 full-time equivalent students with more than 55% high-level
work. These colleges will be established with corporate status and
manage their own affairs in terms of employing staff, owning their
own buildings and equipment. Planning and resources overall will be
the responsibility of a new body: Polytechnics and Colleges Funding
Council (PCFC). The Secretary of State is accused by educationalists
'in the field' of creating a tripartite system of higher education and
creating a two-year planning blight since local authorities are
unlikely to wish to invest top-up funds in organizations they are

8

shortly to lose. Concern is expressed at the further centralist measures and at the treatment of the NAB in that the White Paper has forestalled the publication of the 'Good management practice report' which the government had itself commissioned. Another worry for colleges is the prospect of asset stripping by some local authorities before their colleges and polytechnics pass to central government control. Plant, equipment and materials could be at risk and this would obviously pose problems for those concerned with managing resources. This problem has been recognized and steps taken to deal with it, although new developments are likely to be affected in the interim period.

The human factor within this debate is very real and cannot be ignored. In terms of the teaching force, due consideration must be given to those people remaining in colleges and sharing the extra duties left behind by former colleagues (it would be a delusion to suggest that the match between redundant staff and outdated courses is exact and finite!). The increased commitments ensuing from all the planning exercises and the coming to terms with developments that current changes in the government's educational policies have created must also be taken into account. All this in the climate of unease and uncertainty that is encountered during periods of rapid change. There are those people within the profession for whom all this is stimulating, exciting and challenging – just the thrust they need to precipitate their next phase of creativity or entrepreneurial drive. For others, such a climate is a sure means of fostering a crisis of self confidence and a drop in morale.

> Having to accept that your existing expertise is no longer needed or valued involves individuals' personal assumptions regarding their own worth, as does perhaps no other aspect of change. Many people experience this with a sense of personal inadequacy. Development of this aspect of the college is a vital process which cannot simply be answered by the provision of courses for staff.
>
> Miller *et al.*[26]

A part of this exercise has been a close re-examination of many routes to vocational and professional qualification – this has been for example the era of BEC, TEC, and subsequently BTEC development with drastic alterations in teaching methods, curriculum and course design and in evaluation and assessment methods with its greatly increased workloads for those staff in colleges concerned with these particular disciplines. It has also been the period during which several professions have taken steps from diploma to degree status bringing their own proliferation of committee work both in and outside the college, new course proposal work, student counselling and personal updating.

It is the era in which a whole new way of looking at college organization is advocated by organizations such as FEU[26] and FESC[27] through their projects on curriculum-led institutional development.

These additional pressures are having to be absorbed against an increasingly unstable background and at a time when promotion prospects for many are at their lowest for many years. It is a period which has seen one of the bitterest disputes over lecturers' salaries. Though salary and conditions of service disputes in the higher and further education sector have not had as much publicity as those of the school sector, nevertheless the dispute is very real to those involved and morale is not improved by current discussions which appear to lead inevitably (as lecturers see it) to a worsening of conditions and a decrease in their professional autonomy.

Unemployment problem initiatives

In many colleges that come within the remit of this analysis all the foregoing factors are being grappled with. At the same time, because of the balance of advanced and non-advanced undertakings, equal or perhaps even greater attention must be paid to the stream of 'initiatives' that have sprung up at the non-advanced end of the spectrum, the 16-19 group as it has come to be termed, in an attempt to find solutions, compromises or palliatives to the ever-increasing youth unemployment problem.

The curtain raiser to this development was the establishment in 1974 of the Manpower Services Commission (MSC) operating under two bodies – the Employment Services Agency (ESA) and the Training Services Agency (TSA).

The first major report from this organization was the Holland Report in 1977[28] which spawned the first of a series of programmes and initiatives (and incidentally the first of an inreasing flood of bewildering acronyms). Between 1977 and 1987 we have encountered YOP, WEEP, STEP, UVP (the latter jointly with the DES), Open Tech., TVEI, RVQ, ATS, RESTART, WOW and JTS just briefly to name the various schemes established by MSC. (For explanation of acronyms see Appendix.)

In 1981 MSC published two consultative documents:

- *A new training initiative:*[29] which was a plea for a coordinated approach to a more fully developed and relevant training

10

programme in Britain, inviting comments from employers, trade unions and the education service.
- *An 'Open Tech' programme:*[30] a proposal to open up the access to further education.

These were followed within six months by a Command Paper:

- *A new training initiative:*[31] *a programme for action:* published by the Department of Employment.

The latter was concerned with the issues raised in both the MSC consultative documents. The ten-point programme embodied in this White Paper placed much emphasis on training, making the country's workforce more effective, competitive and relevant to the needs of new technology and the demands of the marketplace. There was a consideration of problems relating to the transition from full-time education to work and proposals for the examination of school curricula identifying a pressing need to increase their relevance to the world of work. There was much preoccupation with the funding of training and considerations of how costs should be met and there was an investment of £1 billion in a one-year Youth Training Scheme for all minimum-aged unemployed school leavers.

January 1984 saw the publication of perhaps the most hotly debated White Paper of all on this subject. *Training for Jobs* (Cmnd 9135) made a transfer of 25% of the funding for non-advanced further education to the MSC and away from the local authority education service a matter of government policy. The reason advanced for its policy was the failure on the part of FE colleges to provide in an appropriate way for the needs of employers.

These 'initiatives' on the part of MSC and the government have brought much acrimonious debate on to the non-advanced further education scene, as well as much anxiety to many of its individual teachers. There has perhaps never been such a strong feeling of injustice, low morale, cynicism while at the same time being faced with the stark realities of the educational climate. These feelings have been expressed in debates in colleges and amongst the representative associations.

The reasons for such a reaction were many and they were the culmination of developments since the setting up of the MSC, whose activities can be variously described as:

- Genuine concern for the state of the nation and its serious economic difficulties.

11

- Meeting the need to produce measures to alleviate the social hardship brought about by increasing unemployment.

Or alternatively as:

- Palliatives and political manoeuvres to mask the inefficiency of the government of the day.
- Policy measures of a centralist government to reduce the power of local authorities via their education budgets.

It is no surprise to find that those in colleges most affected by these developments tend towards the less charitable interpretations. There is a real concern amongst further education practitioners and managers about what they perceive as the destructive effect that current government policies seem to be having. There is considerable feeling that a short-sighted approach is being taken and that political arguments are replacing educational considerations.

Since *Training for jobs* was a Command Paper rather than a consultative document, it apparently left little room for comment by those people in further education who saw their very *raison d'être* being threatened. Already pushed hard towards an acceptance of various MSC programmes and busily engaged in submitting pilot schemes in attempts to attract MSC funding into their financially hard-pressed colleges, they now saw the threat of 25% of their funding being passed over to MSC control. If they refused to cooperate willingly there was a real danger that they would either be coerced into 'cooperation' or that their students, already declining in numbers for various reasons, would be attracted instead into private sector schemes with the likely consequence that courses would fold because minimum enrolment numbers could not be maintained.

Many of the criticisms against colleges were principally that their existing relationships with industry were poor. The fact that, in many cases, these criticisms were unfounded and the MSC organizers, on their own admission, often lacked experience and could not guarantee a better performance, did not make the pronouncements of the White Paper any more palatable. NATFHE protested loudly on behalf of its members and the LEAs and the FE service were in bitter dispute with the government for many months.

A degree of compromise was eventually achieved under the MSC Chairmanship of Bryan Nicholson, successor to Lord Young, with the setting up of a Review Group on work-related NAFE[32] to examine means of bridging the gap between the LEAs and government on MSC involvement in NAFE. This new body, Manpower

Services Commission – Local Authority Associations' Group on Work-Related Non-Advanced Further Education (MSC-LAAS WRNAFE!), was formed in February 1985 to consider how to plan non-advanced further education in the colleges and allocate the money channelled through MSC as a result of the *Training for Jobs* White Paper. Its terms of reference were:

1   To assess in broad terms the present range of LEA provision for work-related NAFE and the existing arrangements for review and change in response to new demands, including arrangements for consultation with employers and trade unions.

2   To consider the development of training policies, trends in the labour market and demographic trends as they affect NAFE in the light of 1 above, and assess what changes in procedures and policies might be necessary to assist in responding to labour market needs and the needs of individuals.

3   To consider what local and national arrangements should be recommended for liaison between LEAs and MSC in planning for NAFE.

4   Similarly, to consider arrangements for consultation with employers and trade unions.

5   To consider how funding channelled through MSC should be managed, taking account of the need to maintain reasonable continuity of provision and to avoid complex administrative procedures.

6   To make recommendations to the Commission and local authority associations by 31 May 1985.

Crown copyright. Reproduced with the permission of the Controller of Her Majesty's Stationery Office.

Agreement was reached whereby local authorities were to produce plans annually for their NAFE provision and the whole process was due to be reviewed in May 1987.

Though one cannot deny the value of undertaking market research and assessment of relevance of courses as implied within the agreement outlined in the first report of this body, colleges may well recoil at the additional work involved. The review group's report was published in May 1985 and the government has accepted its findings. The peace, however, is an uneasy one, with the situation being carefully watched by interested educationalists. The formal watchdog is the Education and Training Group – a group which established itself as a result of a decision of the Area Manpower Board Members conference convened by AMA in September 1984. This group, made up of LEA elected members, NATFHE, NUS and careers service representatives, monitors activities and acts as an information disseminator for the education sector.

Other developments include the appointment of Lord Young as Employment Secretary, the publication in April 1985 of *Education and training for young people*[33] containing among other policy items the extension of YTS to a two-year scheme and the establishment of the 'Review of vocational qualifications' under the aegis of MSC.

RVQ has itself had a mixed reception – one of the main criticisms being that there is an imbalance between employer and professional representation on its council. The aims of RVQ are to identify

> the strengths and weaknesses of the present arrangements for certifying vocational achievement and to specify objectives for an improved system and to make recommendations on how the objectives can be met by establishing a new body responsible for implementing change (NCVQ), by designing a national framework for vocational qualifications and by establishing arrangements for specifying standards of competence required in employment.[20]
> *Crown copyright. Reproduced with the permission of the Controller of Her Majesty's Stationery Office.*

Work is progressing under a series of subject-oriented project groups and a working group on assessing competence. The new framework of qualifications should be operational by 1991 if present time-scales are maintained. Some examining bodies are starting to alter their qualifications even in advance of NVCQ requirements and colleges are being urged to do their own forward planning.

At the time of writing the situation brought about by the so-called initiatives, to meet the needs firstly of changing patterns in the workforce and secondly changing educational needs of the population in general is still far from being resolved. The climate is still extremely volatile with the attendant stresses that rapid change, financial instability and uncertainty inevitably foster.

Summary

An attempt has been made to chart the major happenings in politics and further and higher education which have brought us to our present position. This has been done largely by reference to the various government and related reports published during the period under review. Such a survey must needs be brief to keep the introductory matter in proportion to the remainder of the text. For fuller information the reader is referred to the reports themselves, details of which are to be found in 'Background reading to Chapters 1 and 2' (see p.162).

References

1 Ministry of Education, *15 to 18, Report of the Central Advisory Council for Education, England*, (Chairman Crowther), vol.1. Report, vol. 2. Surveys, HMSO, 1959-60.

2 Committee on Higher Education, *Higher education*, (Chairman Robbins), Cmnd 2154, HMSO, 1963.

3 Ministry of Education, *Technical education*, advisory panel report, Cmnd 9703, HMSO, 1956.

4 Ministry of Education, *Better opportunities in technical education*, Cmnd 1254, HMSO, 1961.

5 Ministry of Labour, *Industrial training*, Cmnd 1892, HMSO, 1962.

6 Department of Education and Science, *Plan for polytechnics and other colleges*, Cmnd 3006, HMSO, 1966.

7 Open University Planning Committee, *Open University*, HMSO, 1969.

8 Ministry of Education, Committee on General Studies, *General studies in technical colleges*, HMSO, 1962.

9 Department of Education and Science, Committee on Day Release, *Day release*, HMSO, 1964.

10 National Association of Schoolmasters, *Technical teacher training*, 2nd. ed., NAS, 1969.

11 Department of Education and Science, *Education: a framework for expansion*, Cmnd 5174, HMSO, 1972.

12 Department of Education, *Rate fund expenditure and rate calls in 1974-5*, Circular 2/74, HMSO, 1974.

13 Confederation of British Industry, Conference Speaker, *Times Educational Supplement*, 22 November, 1985, 16.

14 'CBI's warnings on HE Green Paper', *NATFHE Journal*, 11, (1), 1986, 8.

15 Department of Education and Science, *Higher education: meeting the challenge*, Cm 114, HMSO, 1987.

16 Treasury and Civil Service Committee, *Government expenditure 1985/86 to 1987/88*, Cm 56, HMSO, 1987.

17 National Economic Development Office and Manpower Services Commission, *Competence and competition*, NEDO, 1984.

18 Manpower Services Commission, *Skills shortages report*, MSC internal paper, 1984.

19 Department of Employment, *Employment: the challenge for the nation*, Cmnd 9474, HMSO, 1985.

20 Manpower Services Commission and Department of Education and Science, *Review of vocational qualifications in England and*

Wales; a report by the working group, (Chairman De Ville), MSC/DES, 1986.

21 Department of Employment, *Training for jobs*, Cmnd 9135, HMSO, 1984.

22 Department of Education and Science, *The Development of higher education into the 1990s*, Cmnd 9524, HMSO, 1985.

23 Industry Year, (1) *Education and industry, industry matters, further education;* (2) *Education and industry, industry matters, initial training of teachers*, Industry Year, Royal Society for the Encouragement of Arts, Manufactures and Commerce, 1986.

24 'White Paper detail makes grim reading', *Education*, 169, (16), 1987, 339.

25 op. cit. 15 29

26 Miller, John *et al., Preparing for change: management of curricular-led institutional development*, Longmans for FEU, 1986, 18.

27 Turner, C.M., *Curriculum-led institutional organisation: a background theoretical paper*, Coombe Lodge, working paper, Information Bank Number 1812, FESC, May 1983.

28 Manpower Services Commission, *Young people and work*, (Chairman Holland), MSC, 1977.

29 Manpower Services Commission, *A new training initiative: a consultative document*, MSC, 1981.

30 Manpower Services Commission, *An 'Open Tech' programme: to help meet adult training and retraining needs at technician and related levels. A consultative document*, MSC, 1981.

31 Department of Employment, *A new training initiative: a programme for action*, Cmnd 8455, HMSO, 1981.

32 Manpower Services Commission/Local Authority Associations Policy Group, *Review group on work-related non-advanced further education, report.* MSC/LAA, 1985. (Quoted in *Education* 15 Feb. 1985, 144.)

33 Department of Education and Science, *Education and training for young people*, Cmnd 9482, HMSO, 1985.

Chapter 2   Issues in further and higher education

Some of the issues referred to briefly in Chapter 1 and of significance during the period under review are discussed in greater detail in this chapter.

The advanced further education pool

The advanced FE pool was introduced in 1959 but expenditure on teacher training and advanced further education has been consolidated into a single combined pool since 1975. The rationale of the pool is that certain educational services are provided by only a limited number of local authorities but are of general benefit and that it is reasonable that expenditure incurred by authorities providing those services should be shared amongst all authorities. Pooling is the device used to achieve this purpose. Every local authority was required to contribute its share to the pool from which *providing* authorities recovered their actual expenditures.

Contributions to and claims from the pool were calculated by a complex series of arrangements set out in Rate Support Grants (Adjustments of Needs Element) Regulations 1976, No. 1939, with several subsequent amendments.

From its inception to the introduction of pool capping the size of the pool grew from a total of £31m to £500m, from 1960 to 1979. This rapid growth reflects the policies of successive governments to expand the provision for higher education. However, a shift from growth to contraction as well as mounting criticism of the unfairness of the system and its effects on individual authority attitudes, possibly fostering extravagance rather than economic efficiency, self-centred aims rather than a national purpose, occasioned a closer examination of procedures and resulted in 1980 in a 'capping of the pool' approaching the exercise from the opposite end.

There was henceforth to be a clear limit set *in advance* on the amount which a local authority could claim from the pool. This required a decision on the total amount to be available for distribution and a method for deciding the sums to be apportioned to individual authorities, leaving each authority the option of topping up the amount spent on advanced FE if it so wished. For the first year the amount was fixed politically and somewhat arbitrarily. For several subsequent years there was enhancement for inflation but this was phased out by 1983-4. This reduced funding – as indeed it was to be for most colleges – led to a closer examination of staff/student ratios, staffing reviews, RACs course approvals and a changed relationship between colleges and their LEAs in respect of estimates and funding.

It soon became apparent that a more refined procedure was required. A DES study group made up of practitioners in the various sectors was set the task of devising a mechanism and a policy for the distribution and funding of advanced further education. One of the major needs expressed was for a national body to formulate guidelines and review provision as an entity. Such a body subsequently emerged in the form of the National Advisory Body for Local Authority Higher Education in England and Wales.

The National Advisory Body for Local Authority Higher Education in England and Wales (NAB)
This body had a long period of gestation. The first suggestions for a central body to plan and coordinate higher education in the maintained sector, to control its financing and provide better links with the university sector were outlined in the Robbins report in 1963 (Cmnd.2154).[1] *Education: a framework for expansion* (Cmnd.5174)[2] referred to the need for improved arrangements for coordination and provision and suggested that the appropriate vehicle was the Local Authorities Higher Education Committee. *Report of the working group on the management of higher education in the maintained sector,* (Chairman Gordon Oakes, Cmnd. 7130)[3] published in 1978, made similar recommendations for a 'national body' to plan, coordinate and finance maintained-sector higher education. In January 1980 in default of action on these recommendations and because the Education Bill, which proposed advanced further education councils, had been lost at the change of government, CLEA set up its higher education group in a move towards the establishment of a forum to plan and coordinate the maintained sector of higher education. The Select Committee on Education, Science and the Arts' *Funding and organization of courses in higher education,* 5th report, (1979-80)[4] recommended 'that a Committee for Colleges and Polytechnics (CCP) should be set up by the Secretary of State to give advice and

make recommendations about the finance, administration and planning of institutions in the maintained sector engaged in Advanced Further Education.'

Sir Keith Joseph finally announced the formal establishment of the National Advisory Body in a written parliamentary reply:

> With the agreement of the local authority associations and after consultation with other interested bodies I have decided to establish a new advisory body in the academic provision to be made in local authority institutions of higher education. The advice this body will provide will assist me in the performance of my statutory duties in relation to the distribution of the advanced further education pool and the approval of advanced courses. The advisory body will comprise a Committee supported by a Board and such sub-committees as the Board may appoint.

It was thus in effect the Oakes Committee, established by a Labour government, which in 1978 formally proposed the National Body and a Conservative government that established it in 1982. The Secretary of State for Education confirmed its permanent continuance in 1984 – its original establishment having been proposed as an interim measure.

Terms of reference for the board and the committee are as set out below:

The board

To receive instructions from and make recommendations to the Committee for Local Authority Higher Education in pursuit of the fulfilment of the Committee's Terms of Reference. In so doing, the Board will:

a. establish such ad hoc groups as the Committee judges necessary to assist with aspects of this task;

b. establish effective liaison with the university, voluntary and direct grant sectors of higher education, with appropriate validating and professional bodies and, as necessary, with representatives of industry and commerce;

c. secure advice from appropriate sources as necessary on the regional and local aspects of local authority higher education.

The committee

1 For the time being and in the light of resources specific for Local Authority Higher Education in England by the Secretary of State after consultation with local authorities, to consider on the basis of recommendations from the Board for Local Authority Higher Education, the

academic provision to be made in institutions in selected fields as decided by the Committee.

2   To advise the Secretary of State, in respect of those fields, on the appropriate use of his powers with regard to the apportionment of the advanced further education pool and to the approval of advanced courses.

3   To monitor the implementation by local authorities and institutions of dispositions made by the Secretary of State in the light of this advice.

4   In formulating this advice, to contribute to a coordinated approach to provision, as necessary in relevant academic fields, between the local authority and the university, voluntary and direct grant sectors of higher education.

5   To undertake or commission such studies or to seek such information as appear necessary for the determination of this advice.

Locke et al.[5]

Shortly after its inception the board conducted a major survey of colleges amassing more information about individual institutions than had ever before been available. It was on the basis of the 'evidence' of this, the first of the NAB's major planning exercises, that the AFE pool allocations for 1984-5 were made. College courses were collected into broad subjects and grouped into programme sectors, 'weightings' being added for various reasons. Subsequent exercises have given rise to further modifications and in November 1985 a new methodology for the distribution of the AFE pool was adopted. This gave rise to added concern within the profession since the already complicated process of calculating a college's allocation was made even more complex and some institutions, notably those providing initial teacher training and those larger institutions with lower percentages of advanced work, suffer greater cuts by this methodology. Frank Griffiths, NATFHE's Education Secretary, explains this aspect in some detail (*NATFHE J.*, Nov. & Dec., 1985).[6&7] There is a general consensus that however funding for further and higher education is organized it cannot be made efficient or truly effective at present funding levels.

Apart from the concern and indeed the effects already felt over the NAB's policies on funding, educationalists affected by its establishment feel a broader concern relating to its wider functions. These arise from the centralist route from which the NAB originated:

the conclusion of the process is the establishment of a national body which will take decisions which not only belong, properly and legally, to local authorities, but which belong to individual institutions themselves. It is understood, in the Department of Education and Science and in educational administration generally, that these developments are illegal.

Locke et al.[8]

The authors suggest there is a different role that the NAB could effectively take, namely that 'of formulating the national problems to which individual institutions propose educational solutions, and to judge and find which solutions proposed are most likely to help solve these problems'. They go on to detail how the board might pursue this exercise, including indicating priorities in its allocation of funds by 'problem budgeting'.

Such an approach might go some way to meeting their criticism and one often expressed by educationalists including a former government minister (Shattock)[9] that there is and has been for many years a lack of real government policy for education based on educational rather than on purely political and financial dictates.

The Leverhulme Programme devoted several of its 17 recommendations to the need for more positive educational policy formulation including the establishment of a higher education policy studies centre to serve as an independent source of advice for the DES and other government departments. It also advocated an 'overarching' body for both the NAB and the UGC to produce a policy for the whole of higher education and to close the great divide of the binary system (see p.24).

Cm 114[10] put an end to all these proposals, however, since the NAB by its dictates is to go out of existence. It has not, on many occasions, been allowed to fulfil the role Sir Keith Joseph assigned to it as an adviser to the Secretary of State (most significantly perhaps in the timing of the White Paper's publication *before* its own good management practice report, commissioned by the Secretary of State!) The White Paper also rejects the proposal for an overarching body and rather than losing the binary system we seem well on the way to a tripartite one!

The Audit Commission
Since 1980 the Audit Commission has been charged with securing 'economy, efficiency and effectiveness in local authorities'. Further education was soon identified as one of the areas for investigation. In 1981 a firm of management consultants was commissioned in an attempt to ascertain how efficiency in FE might be assessed. As a result of the consultants' study the Department of the Environment Audit Inspectorate published in 1983, *Colleges of FE: guide to the measurement of resource efficiency*.[11] This guide identified a number of performance indicators and was used by the firms which conduct local authority audits under the direction of district auditors to examine 165 FE colleges.

In 1985 the Audit Commission published *Obtaining better value from further education*[12] which purports to report the findings of the college surveys and which broadly suggested that £50m per annum savings might be made with better marketing and more effective cost control of operations.

It met with strong criticism in the national and professional press, largely on the grounds of deficiencies in the documentation, the contradictory nature of some of the recommendations and the fact that contentious issues involving academic and professional judgements were dealt with tactlessly.

In spite of the critical attitude taken by FE managers and practitioners to the Audit Commission Report it is a significant factor in the current educational scene in that it highlights the requirement for colleges and local authorities to be accountable in rather more precise ways than has been the case heretofore (it points up the need to record more carefully basic management data in terms of funding, teaching and support staff and students) to enable them to operate more efficiently. This is not to deny the validity of the criticism levelled at the simplistic approach used by the commission, reaction to which has been vindicated to some extent by comments in the HMI report published in the spring of 1987 which reports finding colleges responsive and flexible, meeting the needs of employers and local communities (*Education,* 6 Mar 1987).[13]

FEMIS
FEMIS may be seen by some colleges as a partial answer to the Audit Commission's demands for more detailed analysis and evaluation of their operations.

'Further Education Management Information System' devised by the staff of the Further Education Staff College is a microcomputer-based system covering aspects of college resource management. It provides the facility for collecting data on academic staffing, timetabling, room utilization, costing and finance, planning and budgeting and student records. Detailed analysis of data is possible and comparison of performance of similar courses and departments within and across colleges. It is consistent with DES, District Audit and the Chartered Institute of Public Finance and Accountancy surveys and analyses. A series of user services is provided to assist with installation, software operations and emergency recovery in the case of database corruption. FEMIS workshops are held regularly at the Staff College to provide instruction and hands-on experience of running the system on a variety of computers.

Use of FEMIS in colleges has caused concern among teaching staffs, especially those members who are particularly union-orientated. There is a fear, somewhat similar to that voiced in response to the Audit Commission report, that too much emphasis is being placed on SSRs as a leading determinant in course provision and that these particular methods of measurement do not make sufficient distinction between efficiency and effectiveness.

The FEU packages do not cater for all the data needed for college evaluation exercises and other in-house and commercial systems are being developed.

FEU

The Further Education Curriculum Review and Development Unit was established in 1977 by the Secretary of State for Education with the aim of making possible a more cohesive and coordinated approach to curriculum development in further education. It became an independent limited company in 1983 and operates from DES at Elizabeth House. Its philosophy is that for curriculum development to be credible and effective, it must arise from research, study and observation out in the field rather than from an isolated think tank. It aims therefore to work in and through colleges and authorities using the following methods:

- Reviewing the range of existing curricula.
- Determining priorities and suggesting improvements.
- Carrying out studies, curriculum experiments and evaluation.
- Disseminating FE curriculum information.

Documentation of its activities has been through a series of publications: project reports, occasional papers and annual reports, originally available free of charge from Elizabeth House; some are now being published by Longmans.

Examples of published works include project reports: *Loud and clear: a study of curriculum dissemination, A basis for choice: report of a study on post-16 pre-employment courses, Active learning: guide to current practice in experiential and participatory learning, Developing social and life skills;* occasional papers on 'The changing face of FE', 'Microelectronics in FE' and 'Computer-aided design in FE'; and research projects on 'Computer literacy for UK shipping management', 'Robotics: guidance for further education' and 'Preparing for Change: the management of curriculum-led institutional developments.'

The Leverhulme Programme of Study into the Future of Higher Education

This project was established by the Society for Research into Higher Education (SRHE) known informally as the Leverhulme programme from the support given to the project by the Leverhulme Trust.

The SRHE itself is a body concerned with the promotion of research and development in higher education and draws its membership across the binary line from universities and institutions from the local authority sector of higher education.

The Leverhulme programme, independent of government pressure, was set up in the early 1980s in an attempt to focus informed opinion and recent research findings on the major strategic options likely to be available to higher education institutions and policy-making bodies in the 1980s and 1990s: 'The need for a major review of HE has been recognized by informed commentators for some time and the financial stringency of recent years has made the matter urgent.' (Williams[14]).

Its findings and deliberations were made available in a series of ten monographs published by the SRHE between 1981 and 1983 which looked at the labour market, the existing adverse climate, resources, professional evaluation, future of research, structure and governance and related topics. The 1983 SRHE conference formed a culmination to the programme taking as its theme 'The future of higher education' and picked up key issues related to the Leverhulme conclusions, the whole being reported in its 19th Annual Conference Proceedings.

Many specific recommendations came out of the various debates which it is not feasible to catalogue here. We would refer readers to the original documentation but it is interesting to highlight one significant suggestion – that there is a commonality of issues facing education on either side of the binary line and that a 'post binary' structure is needed, that there should be a national commission established overlapping both the NAB and the UGC with a remit to produce a 'public and sophisticated plan for all higher education'. It should be acknowledged, however, that in some instances policy decisions have to be made too quickly and cannot wait for the completion of research.

As these paragraphs are being written, the White Paper *Higher education: meeting the challenge* has just been published, rejecting the suggestion for an overarching body. Its terms, in effect, split higher and further education provision three ways rather than close the existing divide and run counter to the main thrust of Leverhulme. The government appears to be prepared to go in a completely opposite direction to that advocated by leading educational professionals and this can do little for morale in further and higher education.

Open College

The proposal to form the Open College was announced by Lord Young, Secretary of State for Employment, in July 1986.

Sheila Innes, formerly head of BBC's Continuing Education Department, has been appointed Chief Executive.

September 1987 saw the launch of the first related television programmes and enrolment on to courses. Courses will eventually be provided up to degree level using open learning delivery systems to widen access to vocational and skills training.

Open College students will be able to study independently for a variety of qualifications validated by such bodies as the Business and Technical Educational Council, City and Guilds of London Institute and the Royal Society of Arts.

Study materials will be delivered via a combination of radio and television broadcasts, texts, videos and audio cassettes. Initially television broadcasts will be for one hour each week day on Channel 4.

Open College will establish a number of Student Support Centres across the country to provide information, learning resources, staff, counselling etc. as a back-up service to formal course materials.

Open College is willing to receive proposals for student support centres from the public sector, voluntary agencies, private companies or training agencies. In some cases a combined provision may be possible with a networked system of databases to keep information up-to-date.

Student funding

There are many anomalies in the present methods for funding students to participate in post-compulsory education. The present structure of financial support for students was established in 1962 as an outcome of the Anderson Committee recommendations and has remained with only minor changes. It is not practicable to detail all the complexities of the system here and for a detailed account the reader is referred to Maureen Woodall.[15]

When introduced, the British system was the envy of students in many countries; in more recent years, however, it has become the subject of much criticism. Criticisms range from the inadequacy of the present levels of student grants to the inequity of a system which includes a division between discretionary and mandatory grants, is means-tested, relates to parental incomes for people up to the age of 25 and in any case makes no legal obligation for the payment of the parental contribution.

The present system favours participants in AFE in preference to part-time courses. It also works against married women's participation in further qualification. Many of these considerations adversely affect course development in terms, for example, of offering more flexible provision, more provision for mature students and for non-advanced work.

The fact that grant levels have not kept pace with recent inflation levels and the present pressures to reduce public expenditure means there is little likelihood of removal of anomalies or improvement of financial support. Indeed considerable attention is being paid to the possibility of introducing student loans. The Secretary of State's 1985 attempts in this direction caused a furore on the political scene. In September 1986, in the university sector, the Vice Chancellors agreed to back a mixed grants/loans system. The NUS felt betrayed by the heads of their institutions who had up to then supported their campaign for a 20% increase in grant levels. At the time of writing a government report has been 'imminent' for a very long time! The White Paper (Cm 114)[16] defers it once more:

> The Government acknowledges that future arrangements for student support will have a bearing on student demand, particularly perhaps on the extent to which demand from mature and part-time students might increase. Student support arrangements are being reviewed separately and the Government's conclusions from that review will be announced in due course. The review will take full account of the importance of maintaining access to higher education by students from all social and economic backgrounds.

Activity within the secretariat, with George Walden, HE Minister, going on fact-finding tours in America and Sweden would suggest that a mixed loans/grants system is favoured by the government.

The MSC is also charged to look into the question of grants for students staying on at school after 16 and an element in their argument may well be that students in sixth form or FE colleges might otherwise be drawing a YTS allowance thus introducing another factor into the debate. (*TES* 13 Sept. 1985).[17]

The announcement that with the introduction of two-year YTS course participants would be paid benefit levels plus expenses met with misgivings from NATFHE and other trade unions.

A Labour Party working party of educationalists recently recommended that all full-time students aged 16-19 should be eligible for a

£27 per week maintenance grant, that mandatory awards for higher education students should be restored by stages but as quickly as possible to at least the real value in 1978-9, that Open University and part-time degree courses should also be covered by a mandatory grant. The report also says that parental contributions should be phased out by the early 1990s. Loans are rejected as likely to deter women and students from poorer families from entering higher education (*Guardian*, 4 Dec. 1985).[18]

If the final decision is one that moves the onus for all or part of the funding of students' post-compulsory education on to the student, two major effects are likely to ensue. One is in terms of the discouragement of taking up further education with the disincentive of a large debt to be repaid, the second in terms of the possible difficulties of repayment of loans in a society where guarantees of gaining employment on completion of study are decreasing and where career prospects and length of working life and earning potential could affect ability to repay. There may, on the other hand, be those students who would welcome the independence from parents that loans would give.

Increased leisure
Though there has been a steady stream of 'initiatives' and schemes – some from the DES but many from the DOE route – particularly in the NAFE sector, the emphasis has been very largely upon the need to better equip the rising generation for the world of work. By comparison very little attention has been paid to the changing needs and the demands to be made by that group of the population who, for various reasons, do and will increasingly turn to further education with requirements that are not work-related. Despite government optimism there is no real indication at the time of writing of a significant downturn in the unemployment figures and even if this were to begin to happen there will be for some years a considerable number of people with increased leisure time – as a result of early retirement, shorter working weeks and periods of unemployment.

> Education and leisure may become the number one industry of the 1990s. Many people will not want the passive spectatorship that many of today's leisure activities offer. They will want to learn. We could be on the threshold of the dream some people have had for years – life long education . . . the whole notion of community education is going to grow. It is our duty to provide education for the whole community.
>
> Wragg[19]

At the higher education end of the spectrum, reduction in the number of university places will mean people who in less pressured years would have gone to university will be taking places in other institutions – a process that will reverberate through the whole system leaving people with considerable abilities 'at the other end of the line'.

Both these issues have far-reaching implications for the curriculum.

Signposts[20] gives a detailed survey of educational provision for the 16-19 age group, the major part of which is devoted to vocational preparation and specific career-orientated educational training with one brief chapter on courses for the unemployed in which it makes the observation that curriculum design work has not, as in work-related courses, been undertaken by national organizations but has been left to the individual colleges.

These courses divide broadly into two groups – those assuming eventual employment incorporating elements designed to make participants more employable, and those aimed at giving assistance to people likely to be unemployed for long periods in enhancing the quality of their enforced leisure time:

> The education and training services have a role to play in relation to making it possible for people to cope with this kind of future. We can help make it possible for people to create their own jobs. One of the most interesting and hopeful recent developments has been the way in which groups of young people have been assisted in setting up their own operations by community education workers, by MSC staff, by voluntary organizations and in a few cases by LEA officers.
>
> Taylor[21]

Such an approach emphasizes the counselling role that college lecturers are being and will increasingly be expected to undertake and the greater need for liaison with other agencies.

Conclusion

This then is the scene in which HE and FE is now set and though these are the issues being faced by college lecturers, senior administrators, managers and principals, they are of no less concern to the librarian. As ensuing chapters will show, it is the authors' view that the college librarian is the manager of a central college learning agency and, as such, has a very direct interest in major issues which influence the college. Some of the schemes and 'initiatives' being introduced into colleges will make very specific demands on libraries and other resource services; in some cases they may affect significantly the nature of the service itself. They must therefore be monitored, anticipated and responded to positively.

References

1   Committee on Higher Education, *Higher education,* (Chairman Robbins), Cmnd 2154, HMSO, 1963.

2   Department of Education and Science, *Education: a framework for expansion,* Cmnd 5174, HMSO, 1972.

3   Department of Education and Science, *Report of the working group on the management of higher education in the maintained sector,* (Chairman Oakes), Cmnd 7130, HMSO, 1978.

4   Select Committee on Education, Science and the Arts, Funding and Organization of Courses in Higher Education, *5th Report 1979-80,* vol.1 Report, HC 787-1, HMSO, 1980.

5   Locke, M. *et al., The colleges of higher education, 1972 to 1982: the central management of organic change,* Critical press, 1985, 157-8.

6   Griffiths, F., 'Funding for inequality', *NATFHE Journal,* 10, (7), 1985, 14-16.

7   Griffiths, F. and Figueira, D., 'NAB's new funding methodology or "subquantum abandoned"', *NATFHE Journal,* 10, (8), 18-19.

8   op cit. 5, 159.

9   Shattock, M., *The structure and governance of higher education,* monograph 52, SRHE, 1983, Chapter 3.

10 Department of Education and Science, *Higher education: meeting the challenge,* Cm 114, HMSO, 1987.

11 Department of the Environment, Audit Inspectorate, *Colleges of further education: a guide to the measurement of resource efficiency,* HMSO, 1983.

12 Audit Commission, *Offering better value from further education,* HMSO, 1985.

13 'FE: your flexible friend', *Education,* 169, (10), 1987, 217.

14 Williams, G. (Programme Director), *Preface to: Resources and higher education,* ed. by Alfred Morris and John Sizer, monograph 51, SRHE, 1982, 2.

15 Woodall, M., 'Financial support for students', in Morris, Alfred and Sizer, John, (eds), *Resources in higher education,* monograph 51, SRHE, 1982.

16 op. cit. 10, 11.

17 'Inquiry to look at grants for students staying on at school after 16', *Times Educational Supplement,* 13 September, 1985, 1.

18 Glenmara, 'Student grants', *Guardian,* 4 December 1985.

19 Wragg, Professor T., 'Managing education in the 1980s', *Coombe Lodge Report,* FESC, 15, (4), 1982, 111.

20 Further Education Curriculum Review and Development Unit,

Signposts: a map of 16-19 educational provision, PR 6, FEU, 1980, rev. edn 1985.

21 Taylor, B., 'Taking the initiative', *Coombe Lodge Report,* FESC, 16, (3), 1983, 110.

Chapter 3   The college

This section deals with two related questions: what kind of an institution is a college in management terms? What are the main management issues in the current period of contraction and uncertainty?

Section I: The college and its management
Who are the college's customers? We pose the question because until recently it was a common assumption that colleges existed as part of the order of things in education. This is no longer the case.

When colleges produced documentation about themselves, for example, as part of a CNAA institutional review, their statement about the college more often than not consisted of a description of the courses currently being run together with the historical context. It seemed that because the aims and objectives of the college are implicit in what is currently being done there is no need to articulate them. This reflects a hangover from a bygone age when colleges had defined areas of work and in some cases protected student intakes. The obvious danger is the actual or implied passivity, the institution will always be responding to change rather than initiating it. This is also reflected in those development plans which appear to be almost exclusively concerned with forecasting student enrolments and whose primary purpose seems to be defence of what we have now.

Yet managers are leaders and leaders must determine the purpose of an enterprise as well as devising strategies to achieve that purpose. To justify an undertaking there must be a need, as those colleges of education closed because of the reduction in the need for trained teachers found to their cost. A need arises because of a want on the part of a person or group of people that should be satisfied. These people are potential customers. So we return to the question, who are the college's customers?

One obvious response would be simply, 'the students'. But this would be misleading because the reasons why students go to college are many and various. In many cases the courses have direct vocational/professional goals where the customer may also be the employer or professional association. Products have to be paid for. If we identify the customer as the one who pays, this could be the student. It could be their parents and/or the grant-aiding authority. Some students are sponsored by industrial firms or commercial organizations. Again it could be argued that since grants come from public funding all taxpayers are to some degree customers. All these groups will have some input into the college.

But what is a college? What kind of organization is it and what function does it perform? The complex and changing relationship between central and local government control is not something we shall be dealing with in detail but it results in a number of inputs in policy, direction and resources. Our survey of recent developments in higher and further education gives ample evidence of this. If we regard education as a process which it is necessary for individuals to experience to achieve various goals then the college can be seen as a system to enable that process to take place.

A systems model for college management
System: 'anything formed of parts placed together or adjusted into a regular and connected whole' *(Chambers Dictionary)*.

The model
Systems models for management identify categories of input and output. Between these are the processes which draw on the inputs and create the satisfactory output. This has been expressed diagrammatically (see Figure 3.1).

Figure 3.1 illustrates a *preliminary* systems model, the inputs and outputs can be changed and the 'labels' will vary according to the type of enterprise. Later in this chapter we shall examine a diagram of the college as a system and in the second part of the book apply the systems approach to the college library which is both a sub-system of the college and also a system in its own right.

Inputs
Environment: gives a wide perspective and sets the organization in context. These contexts will vary according to the nature of the organization. For a college the social, political and economic factors are of obvious importance while technology and marketing have recently assumed an increased significance.

Figure 3.1 A preliminary systems model for an enterprise

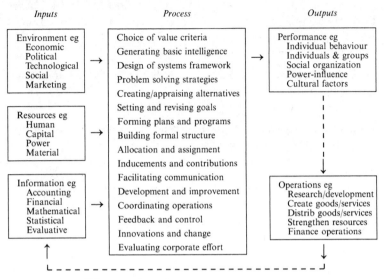

Source: Academy of Managment Journal[1]

Resources: colleges now experience an increasing element of political influence via resource provision (or the lack of it). They also have to consider a change in the balance between the human resource and other resource inputs. Traditionally the human academic/teacher resource has been predominant both in cost and influence. Now this is being significantly modified by two factors, one an input, the other a process:

(a) *Information technology* – the combination of the information and technology inputs has provided a means to change:

(b) the process of *communication and learning* with a consequent effect on the role and proportion of the teaching force in relation to other learning resources.

Another factor is the increasing need to find alternative sources of income to the public purse which leads in turn to the input of other influences.

Information: this will be from two sources: external agencies and evaluative feedback from the institutional processes and operations. Colleges are used to the first source, particularly from governmental and professional agencies, often requiring a response from the institution. The need for evaluation and consequent feedback is something which is coming increasingly to the fore.

Outputs

Operations: covers the basic activities of the institution. In colleges these are becoming more complex and diverse, not least because of the changing nature of the inputs mentioned above.

Performance: has to do with:

● The professional behaviour of individuals and groups within the college.
● The corporate standing of the institution.

Both must be assessed by performance measures and this information fed back to improve the processes and the outputs.

Processes

It is important to distinguish between *processes* and *operations*. A glance at the two groups makes this obvious. Processes enable operations to be carried out efficiently leading to satisfactory performance. Processes are active; they involve choice, design, creativity, planning, decision-making, communication, coordination, innovation and evaluation. This is where the 'art' of the manager is most evident. Managers are agents for change even if they do not always admit to the fact. They must make crucial decisions with regard to the relationships within the system and their role in it. Nothing stands still and if they are sensitive to change they will be constantly modifying the design and operation of their enterprise. To this must be added the human response within the organization to change, experiment, innovation and sometimes, in the college context, to decline.

The more one tries to systematize, the more categories are created and the more boundaries exist. Contact and interaction takes place at the boundaries. They can be a source of resistance or the point of development. Adjusting the system is a process of defining these boundaries, modifying and redefining them.

The college

How can we translate this into college terms? Davies and Morgan[2] identify four models of organization in higher education:

● Bureaucratic
● Collegial
● Political
● Organized anarchy

The bureaucratic model assumes a formal organizational structure, the other three are more flexible, participatory and non-authoritarian. The collegial model assumes consensus decision making by academics with no decisive administrative role. It assumes there will be sufficient cooperation, commitment and resources to enable participatory decision making to be successful without having recourse to hierarchical structures, academic or administrative. The political model is set in a state of perpetual conflict focusing upon issues brought forward by interest groups with different goals. It proceeds by using the decision-making machinery to translate the pressures of these groups into action. The organized anarchy model is when the institution lacks common goals and there is ambiguity and inconsistency in its operation. It introduces decentralization and its formal mechanisms allow participants to pose preferences and air grievances. The success of the head of the institution depends on his ability to have sufficient tactical skill to influence decisions.

These models reflect a period when there was a move towards openness in college government reflected in the constitutions of academic boards following the Weaver Report. None of these types exist in isolation, the basic model is bureaucratic, the other three represent features all or some of which are present within a college. The degree to which they are present may vary according to the nature of the college or events at a particular time which provoke a response.

Latcham and Cuthbert[3] have attempted to develop a systems model for college management. It is interesting to compare their scheme of inputs, processes and outputs (Figure 3.2) with the model quoted earlier in the chapter.

Figure 3.2   Inputs, outputs and processes of the college system

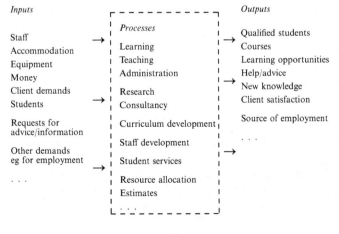

Figure 3.2 is a much simpler diagram. Because it has identified the central process as *learning* it works outwards from that point. It fails to classify or sub-divide under the three main headings of 'inputs', 'outputs' and 'processes'. In consequence, it does not distinguish between the types of input or the relationship between them. Environmental inputs are mixed up with resources, and informational inputs are not covered except as requests for information *not* inputs into the college. It is important to notice the distinction each draws between 'processes' and 'outputs'. In Figure 3.1 the outputs, although covering distribution of goods and services, are essentially the performance and operation of the enterprise. Latcham and Cuthbert include many of these in their processes, regarding outputs as those aspects which go out from the college. Their processes may be adequate for educational activities but they are extremely limited in management terms. The term 'administration' seems to cover many different types of activity. Finally it should be noted, as Figure 3.1 shows, that information and understanding gained from the performance and operation outputs can be fed back as an information input into the organization.

Structures
The complexity of college management is compounded by the interplay between a bureaucratic structure of senior and middle managers and the participative model of committees and working parties. The nature of the personnel and the operation, together with a long tradition of debate, have led to college constitutions which emphasize the importance of structures to enable this to happen.

Figure 3.3 is a model of the committee and management structure of a college. It is not any individual college but includes the features common to many. What immediately stands out is the parallel strands of committee structure and line management. Some colleges attempt to merge the two, inserting the Principal between the Board of Governors and the Academic Board and, less frequently, the Deans/Heads of Departments between the Academic Board and Course Committees. It is interesting to note that some structures acknowledge the presence of informational/advisory units working directly to senior management outside the committee structure.

This situation has in it the seeds of potential dissension and difficulty. Larger colleges have a greater number of courses which leads to a proliferation of infrastructure. Sometimes colleges have developed the maturity to stand back and look at themselves. One college that did so identified some of the limitations of this type of decision-making machinery:

Figure 3.3 College management structure

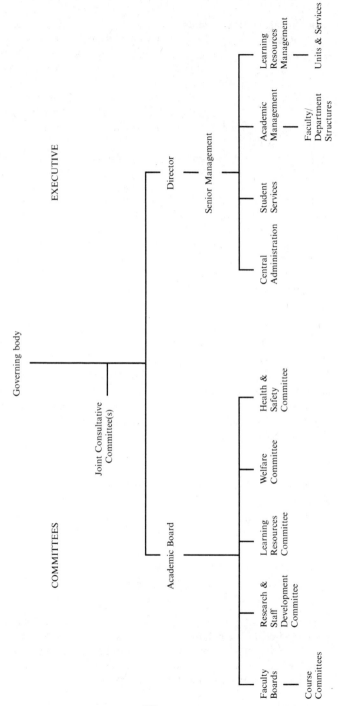

a   In some cases standing committees/sub-boards lacked executive authority: the system allowed some of the chairmen to be elected and those elected were not necessarily senior members of staff or members of the Board of Studies, with a consequent weakening of accountability to the Board.

b   The structure was, in places, ill-suited to achieving properly co-ordinated planning, for example in relation to in-service activities. A more extreme example relates to the co-ordination of learning resources in the college.

c   Delays could be caused by the requirement that only approved minutes of standing committees could be submitted to the Board of Studies.

d   There was no provision for the emergence of a plan of academic development for the institution and no procedures for the determination of priorities.

e   There was no clearly articulated policy of course monitoring and evaluation and no procedures for ensuring that such monitoring and evaluation took place. In consequence the accountability of departments and of sub-boards to the Board of Studies was not fully explicit.

To summarize, the management difficulties experienced were lack of ability to take effective action, accountability, difficulties with coordinated planning, delay, inability to plan ahead, lack of appraisal. No institution can hope to succeed with these weaknesses within its system. This college had taken the first major step of defining the problem and looking it squarely in the face. This was the prelude to a major institutional restructuring to address the problems that had been identified. The success of this exercise was reflected in the positive comments made by the validating body at the next institutional review.

College management and the committee process
We have come to the point in colleges where circumstances are requiring adjustments to be made to the balance between activities of managers and the committee structure. This was discussed by Dr Noel Thompson[4], Under Secretary, Department of Education and Science in a paper given at a Coombe Lodge Conference. Speaking on the topic 'College government up to date' he had this to say about effective management in FE colleges:

> I suppose that my attitude to the somewhat esoteric subject of governance is fundamentally conditioned by the belief that it is not an end in itself, merely a means of promoting good and effective management in further education. It should be about the management of resources – staff, building, equipment – and the effectiveness of the response of the FE

system to changing needs. It should be concerned with the requirement to monitor quality and produce value for money – in broad terms – for ratepayers and taxpayers. Its first and foremost concern is not with staff involvement and democratic consultation (important though they are) but with establishing a framework within which education can be provided effectively and as economically as possible in response to developing needs and demands.

Judged against this concept, the reforms introduced by the Weaver Report probably placed too much emphasis on structures and too little on the principles of management. It is perfectly possible to have structures which operate according to the model articles and the principles of the Weaver Report, and yet to have wasteful educational provision – and poor management at authority and institutional levels.

Whilst it would be much too sanguine to expect the structure of college governance to ensure good and economical provision, it should encourage it by establishing a framework within which responsibilities are clearly defined and effective management can flourish.

While we should not accept Thompson's limited definition of management, we ignore the challenge to manage effectively at our peril. The message is clear: either we promote efficient management and innovation or it will be done for us.

Section II: College management in times of contraction and uncertainty
Colleges are public sector institutions, part of a national system, locally administered, deriving its income very largely from public funds. They have over the years developed a management style and rationale of their own. Although colleges are facing change, uncertainty and contraction they meet these challenges from the standpoint of this management tradition. It is necessary to look at the main features of college management at a time of retrenchment. There is great variety in institutional environments. Historical development, local authority attitudes, differential treatment by funding bodies, the profile of the student body, shifts in student demand are but some of the factors. There has always been an element of uncertainty but this is now present to a markedly greater degree in planning course deployment, patterns of enrolment and budgetary levels. This contrasts strongly with the relatively stable or expansionist period of the 1960s and early 1970s.

The causes of institutional decline can be internal or external to the institution. They may be caused primarily either by political or economic/technical conditions. Institutional decline can develop from any of these factors or a combination of them.

1   *Internal decline* – the institution loses its way:

● Lack of leadership.
● Inability to respond to changing patterns of demand.
● Overpowerful second-tier management (HOD level).
● Lack of new blood.
● Frustration of younger staff.
● Failure to implement proper programmes of course and staff development/appraisal.
● Falling numbers/quality of student intake.
● Poor utilization of resources, especially those directly relating to the learning process.

2   *External pressures*

● Imposed financial constraints.
● Inflation.
● Centralization of planning and increased governmental direction.

This leads to:

● Reductions in student intake targets.
● Direction of course provision.
● Reduction of manpower.
● Performance appraisal.
● Changed balance of central/local government control.
● Other pressures: requirements of validating bodies, more stringent demands from sponsoring bodies.

In many cases the features in group 1 are in direct response to the pressures from group 2. At one end of the continuum there is a belt-tightening exercise, an 'efficiency drive'. Administrative costs are cut, staff–student ratios increased, purchases of materials and equipment are curtailed, an attempt is made to generate alternative sources of income.

As the pressure becomes more severe course options are discontinued, whole courses are cut and manpower is shed, usually through cutback on new appointments, redeployment and early retirement.

At the most extreme there is a programme of closures and mergers with policies to remove staff and the planned disposal of assets. The varying causes of decline in public organizations were surveyed by Levine.[5] Table 9 of his paper deals with institutions of higher education, identifying categories of contraction and indicating possible causes and responses. British higher education can readily identify with the first three of these categories, the most extreme example being the cutback in teacher education in the mid-1970s and the merger/closure programme faced by many colleges of education (see Figure 3.4).

Figure 3.4 Varieties of contraction

Category	Most common causes	Characteristic institutional response
1. Slowed institutional growth; possibility of contraction	Externally imposed fiscal constraints, e.g. recession, government spending limits Stable enrolments or decline in enrolment growth rate Inflation above rate of budget increase	Efficiency measures Deferral of planned programmes and buildings Institutional self-study Increased student marketing efforts Increased fund-raising activities
2. Moderate 'temporary' contraction	Externally imposed budget cuts High rates of inflation Decline in enrolment	Intensified efficiency and productivity measures Some staff development/ redeployment Deferral of certain types of expenditure (principally one-time cuts) Programme reviews as basis for selective cuts Intensified student marketing and fund-raising activities Early retirement policies
3. Substantial contraction over relatively short time	Fiscal crisis, e.g. severe recession or depression or fiscal solvency Sharp decline in enrolments Reorganization/merger of institutions	Crisis personnel policies; redundancies; redeployment Suspension of capital expenditures Intensive mission/ programme studies Closure of units and courses Explicit personnel and recourcing policies
4. Long-term contraction	Permanent state of uncertainty surrounding institutional viability Organizational, political or economic entropy	Programme closures Heavy focus on personnel policies Planned disposal of assets

Source: Levine, Table 9.

This situation would have been undreamt of before 1972. It is now a reality which all have to live with and many have experienced at first hand. We also have to come to terms with the fact that what might at first have appeared to be an uncomfortable but finite interlude is almost certainly here to stay. It is unlikely that in the foreseeable future administrators at local and national level will be prepared to make long-term commitments about the level of support for post-compulsory education. The increased degree of institutional dependence on central planning is unlikely to be matched by a corresponding increase in rational long-term strategies for higher and further education.

In the present situation of contraction more insecurity is generated. The expected institutional response would appear to be more conflict with increased political activity. However, an external threat may concentrate the institutional mind wonderfully and submerge internal dissension in the cause of mutual survival. Such a mood may not last once the crisis has passed but it may offer the senior management a rare opportunity to develop rational and imaginative policies. Unfortunately this opportunity may arise at the very moment when the college leaders are too preoccupied to seize it. In these situations so much depends on the drive, initiative, energy and leadership flair of the principal.

However the senior management may wish to develop a systematic model to assist in the creation and execution of effective policy, there are attitudinal and historical barriers to achieving this. Academic and professional teachers have been insulated from the pressures from outside the college. They have a tradition of professional independence. They seek, and expect others to accept, goals and motivation from within their own teaching and research. Their loyalties are to their department. If change or contraction has to occur, the common reaction is to assume it will happen somewhere else in the system.

Morgan and Davies[6] in the research study which formed the basis of their paper found that there were considerable external pressures for institutions to develop corporate internal management policies. Where senior management attempted to do this there was usually conflict and disagreement which hindered satisfactory progress. They observed the following tendencies in the institutions they studied:

- Joint policy decisions are slow and problematic to make.
- Decisions which are carried through are usually partial, short-range and based on compromise.
- Policy decisions and criteria have to be attacked over and over again before a conventional wisdom gets established.

- More institutional bureaucracy is created, in the sense of more participant involvement, more requests for information to more executives, more referrals of decisions for sub-committee consideration etc.
- The academic finds himself in several concurrent dilemmas: he doesn't like meetings yet he must generate or attend them to preserve his interests and influence, the direction and substance of his plans; he does not wish to spend too much time himself on planning matters, yet he is reluctant to trust others, including administrators; he wishes to plan in the sense of having a stable framework in which to operate, yet he resents being constrained by a substantive plan; he wants a power fixer on whom he can rely to sort out difficult issues, yet he resents the growth of power centres which are beyond the effective control of himself and his colleagues.
- Policy decisions, given the economic realities, environmental uncertainties and political context, may increasingly be concerned with the marginal decision consistent with a very broad, loose framework rather than the grand fixed strategy of a development plan. Points of specificity in planning may be possible on particular issues, but this in itself does not remove the anarchy trap.
- Difficulties with planning and policy making originate with questions of reluctance and inability of participants to plan, namely to imagine the future of the institution as a whole. The role of the rector or central planner would thus seem to be as much concerned with creating an appropriate psychological climate in which participants can be creative, as with the more conventional technical aspects of information collection and analysis.

It is difficult to engage in corporate planning within college because most of the participants are reluctant to engage in the process. They are unable to visualize the institution as a whole. They are unable to formulate college-based objectives and develop strategies to achieve them.

Note: The impact of the government White Paper on higher education (Cm 114) April 1987

The government White Paper, *Higher education: meeting the challenge*[7] lays stress in its introduction on improvements in efficiency by:

> improvements in institutional management
> changes in the management of the system
> the development and use of performance indicators

Its major reform is the proposal to remove higher education from LEA control. In justifying this, the White Paper says of management:

> It is widely acknowledged that the present relationship between local authorities and their polytechnics and colleges can and often does inhibit good institutional management. It also inhibits the desirably closer

relationship between institutions and industry and commerce through consultancy and other services.

Many local authorities apply to their higher education institutions inappropriate detailed controls, some of which are designed for much smaller institutions or other services.

The governors, directors/principals and other senior staff of many polytechnics and colleges are prevented from managing their financial and staffing resources to best effect, and from developing to the full, maturity and responsibility appropriate to higher education institutions.

This is a fundamental step in the management of post-compulsory education, the separation of the control and management of higher and further education and the requirement that institutions of higher education shall:

- Be given more autonomy and required to manage themselves more efficiently (note in particular the reference to performance indicators and the clear emphasis on links with commerce and industry).
- Be subject to more centralized control without the checks and balances of an intermediate level of government.

Only time will tell whether this move will provide the stimulus for strong, imaginative and effective management in those institutions to which it applies.

References

1 'Administrative strategy for a graduate school of administration', *Academy of Management Journal,* December, 1967.
2 Davies, J. and Morgan, A.W., 'Management of higher education institutions in a period of contraction and uncertainty', in *Approaches to post-school management,* Open University with Harper & Row, 1983.
3 Latcham, D. and Cuthbert, R., 'A systems approach to college management', *Coombe Lodge Report,* FESC, 11, (14), 1979, 589-93.
4 Thompson, N., 'College management up to date', in 'College government in the 1980s', *Coombe Lodge Report,* FESC, 16, (12), 1983.
5 Levine, C.H., 'Organizational decline and cutback management', *Public Administration Review,* July/August, 1978, 316-25.
6 op. cit. 2.
7 Department of Education and Science, *Higher education: meeting the challenge,* Cm 114, HMSO, 1987.

Chapter 4   Educational technology and educational objectives

Certain threads have run through our review of colleges and the way they operate. These include the need for effective management, the development of systems, setting the right objectives, innovation, the importance of feedback and evaluation. If we see the college as a system, within it there are a series of sub-systems; one such example is the library. However, the most pervasive will be the course or a departmental/school structure which exists to run (or participate in) a group of courses.

A student entering on a course takes part in a process which should enable him to attain certain educational objectives. This process is learning. To achieve this we need to make resources available. These resources include personnel, learning materials, equipment, accommodation. The personnel will include levels of professional expertise necessary to plan and develop the course as well as to operate it. These may be identical but usually there will be additional inputs at various management levels (and perhaps from outside the college) at the stages of development and later at evaluation and review.

The effective operation of the college that we have discussed earlier will depend upon its output of satisfied students (although one must accept that 'satisfaction' is a term that requires further definition particularly in today's changing situation). The satisfaction of the student, whether expressed only in terms of examination success or in some wider context (either personal or from employers' responses), will depend upon the quality of learning which in turn depends upon the operation of the course.

Using Latcham and Cuthbert's[1] diagram of the course as a system (Figure 4.1) we can see how the aspects mentioned at the beginning apply. We are concerned with: a systematic approach to learning; setting the right objectives; effective management of the learning situation; the implementation of innovation; monitoring and feedback. These we take to be the true province of educational technology. It is not our intention to discuss educational technology in detail, however it seems so essential to the functioning of the library in the college that a brief description of its main features and purpose as we see it is included. It forms a bridge between our consideration of the college and the library. It reinforces the emphasis on the need for a systematic approach to realize stated objectives.

Figure 4.1 The individual course seen as a system

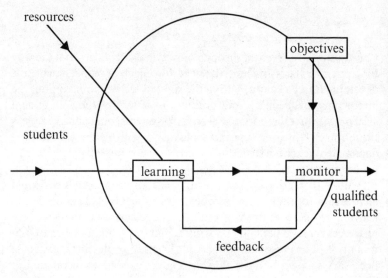

There is an extensive literature on the subject which the reader is advised to consult if he wishes to pursue it in more detail. In particular he is referred to Percival and Ellington's *Handbook of educational technology*,[2] to whose early chapters we are greatly indebted.

What is educational technology?

The nature of the subject and the current state of the art is a matter for constant discussion among educational technologists themselves. Because it is a process, an approach to methods of learning and a spur to innovation it is right and necessary that this should be so. Although the application of educational technology may be continuously modifying, its general principles are capable of definition. Compare the following definitions:

1 Educational technology is the development, application and evaluation of systems, techniques and aids to improve the process of human learning. *Council for Educational Technology, UK*

46

2   Education technology is the application of scientific knowledge about learning, and the conditions of learning, to improve the effectiveness and efficiency of teaching and training. In the absence of scientifically established principles, educational technology implements techniques of empirical testing to improve learning situations.

National Centre for Programmed Learning, UK

3   Educational technology is a systematic way of designing, implementing and evaluating the total process of learning and teaching in terms of specific objectives, based on research in human learning and communication and employing a combination of human and non-human resources to bring about more effective instruction.

Commission on Instructional Technology, USA

They are all concerned with improving the process of human learning. They are concerned with identifying objectives, designing strategies to achieve those objectives, applying a systems approach, reacting positively to innovation, ensuring feedback and evaluation.

Educational technology and audio-visual aids

Education by its very nature is a major user of the technology of information. This has been true through the ages and covers both materials and equipment. In recent years there has been a rapidly increasing diversity of formats in which information is provided together with a range of hardware. This hardware is both 'passive' in facilitating access to existing software or 'active' because it allows one either to create new learning materials or interact with what is already there (e.g. microcomputers).

With such a varied array of equipment and materials constantly being added to, it followed that:

- Lecturers would seek to use them to reinforce their lectures/instruction.
- College management concerned at the level of recurrent investment from annual revenue budgets would seek to develop a form of organization which safeguarded its security, promoted its availability and (in the case of equipment) ensured that it was in working order.

A model for the management of learning materials already existed in the library. An 'audiovisual-aids unit' was often set up with an emphasis on hardware. Software might also be included or transferred to the library. Because of the existence of these units and the emphasis on educational hardware in the early and mid 1970s college lecturers identified this service with educational technology. College lecturers sometimes say, 'I use education technology in my lectures' when they mean 'I use audio-visual aids'.

That such a unit will underpin teaching in a college is undeniable. It is an important aspect of educational technology, particularly in regard to production facilities. The unit can be used in conjunction with lecturing staff to support a number of activities including making in-house learning materials, micro-teaching and developing simple production and study skills techniques for students. However, it is obvious that while these activities are an important and necessary part of the operation in no way do they equate with the breadth of the definitions of educational technology given earlier. Each of the definitions is concerned with ways in which education and training could be improved by a systematic consideration of *all* aspects of the design of teaching/learning situations.

This interpretation equates educational technology with the entire technology of education. It can be argued that its major role is to improve efficiency in the teaching/learning process. Percival and Ellington[3] suggest that this can manifest itself in a number of ways:

   (a) Increasing the quality of learning, or the degree of mastery.
   (b) Decreasing the time taken for learners to attain desired goals.
   (c) Increasing the capacity of teachers in terms of the number of learners taught, without reducing the quality of learning.
   (d) Reducing costs, without affecting quality.

Educational technology requires a systematic approach and apropriate, clearly defined goals which are achievable and enable the success of the operation to be measured. It is an approach that should be central to the college's way of working. It follows logically on from our analysis of the college as a system. It provides a consistent thread between the college system and the course sub-system. It also provides an interface between other sub-systems such as the library and computer units and the learning process.

Approaches to teaching and learning
In Figure 4.1 we showed the course as a system. One of the major inputs was *'resources'*. What resources are input and how they are deployed depends on the approach to teaching and learning. For the purposes of this book we will identify only two broad categories: the teacher/institution-centred approach and the student-centred approach.

The teacher/institution-centred approach
In this approach, which still predominates in our colleges, the teacher

gives the subject matter to a group of students. This subject matter has been laid down in a syllabus and 'interpreted' by the teacher. Classes will be timetabled; teaching will be largely 'face-to-face'; assessment, usually by written examination, will be at the end of the course.

In such a system the institution and the teacher make almost all the decisions about mounting and operating the course. The institution decides the length of sessions, when and where it will meet and who will teach it. The teacher makes the tactical decisions as to how the syllabus is to be covered, the relative weighting to be given to each section, and the level at which it is to be treated. The student usually has little to contribute to these decisions. His role is to respond to the teacher, adapting his learning style to the approach of the teacher and the constraints of the institution.

Advantages of the teacher-centred approach

Such an approach has the merits of being relatively straightforward and easy to administer. It is accepted and understood by the great majority of staff and students. It allows for fairly efficient use of resources, staff, accommodation and equipment. It must also be remembered that within this strategy there can be considerable flexibility in the provision of different learning situations. Revision and remedial sessions can be given. The teacher is clearly central throughout, his experience with the learners is crucial. In situations where strong leadership is required, such as with weak or inexperienced students, this knowledge of the class is essential in determining the most appropriate teaching method.

Shortcomings of the teacher-centred approach

In spite of its long tradition and widespread acceptance the strong central control of the teaching/learning is not always easy to justify. While it can point to many successes it could be argued that these would have been achieved whatever the system and at the expense of many who have had less fortunate results in further and higher education.

A teacher-centred approach has considerable administrative convenience and acceptance by both teachers and students. Nevertheless, it has considerable limitations on *educational* grounds. It places tremendous dependence on the skill and ability of the teacher – a great asset when he is talented and dedicated but presenting major difficulties if he is not.

These limitations may be summarized as:

1   *Interpreting the syllabus:* many syllabi are written in vague terms. The responsibility for what is taught often rests almost entirely with the teacher. If problems arise he has only his own experience and intuition to rely on.

2   *Structuring the content:* with a taught class the common structure which is used is unlikely to be suited to all the individual students. This problem obviously increases with larger classes. The scope for variation to meet the needs of individual students is severely limited.

3   *'Pace':* this can only be appropriate to part of the class with the twin dangers of outpacing the slow-learners and being too slow for the high-fliers. Related to this is the amount of reinforcement and revision that can be built in to a teacher-centred course. Even if this is allowed for, to some extent, when the course is planned it is often the first thing to be sacrificed if teaching time is lost or the class is behind with the syllabus.

4   *Limitation of teaching methods:* in further and higher education the lecture is still the predominant method. Tutorials and seminars which are designed to vary the approach can become mini lectures if not handled properly.

5   *Timetabling:* the problems that can arise here are:
● The standard one-hour periods and the tendency for lectures to fit this slot even though the optimum duration for a lecture may be half this length of time.
● The difficulty of giving proper attention to problems faced by individual learners. Tutorials or revision periods may not coincide with a problem arising which requires more immediate attention.

The student-centred approach

The key features of this approach are flexibility, variety of learning styles, a more supportive and less dominant role for the institution. (*Note:* less dominance does not mean that the institution's role is unimportant.) The student-centred approach can operate at different levels of education and lead to the development of systems of more open learning designed to reduce the conventional barriers of educational opportunity, enabling a potential student of any age or background to study at times and places which suit him. In other words it is designed to meet needs of the individual rather than the requirements of the institution.

It is possible to identify at least three basic patterns of organization:

- Institution-based systems.
- Local systems.
- Distance learning systems.

Percival and Ellington[4] describe them as:

1 *Institution-based systems:* Here the students work at a particular institution with learning facilities and tutor help being provided by the institution on an 'open-access' basis, and the students attending the institution for study at times and at a pace which suits them. A popular system of this type is the *Keller Plan.*

2 *Local systems:* Here, the host institution sets out to offer the student the facilities normally associated with a correspondence course and to back this up with on-the-spot institutional support. Such systems are aimed specifically at members of the local population whose personal situations render it difficult or impossible for them to conform to the rigid restraints of the formal education system. The student does not have to attend college on a regular timetabled basis, and may use a range of individualized learning facilities, both in and out of college. As in institution-based systems college-learning facilities are made available on an open-access basis. An example of this type of system is *Flexistudy,* which is becoming increasingly popular in the UK, especially in the field of further education.

3 *Distance learning systems:* Here, most of the learning takes place away from the host institution. Individualized learning materials are provided for the student, and tutorial help may be made available through correspondence with the institution or via a local tutor (or both). Self-help groups organized by students in a particular geographical area may also spring up. The best known example of a distance-learning system is the *Open University* in the UK.

As with the teacher-centred approach there are advantages and disadvantages and the relative importance of these will depend upon a number of factors. These include the nature and level of education involved, characteristics of the learner, factors relating to the host institution or body.

Advantages of the student-centred approach
The main advantages may be summarized as:

1 Course units are designed to be student-centred, allowing for a variety of approaches to the same material. This permits variation in the order in which assignments are tackled and the pace of learning.

2 There will usually be a set of behavioural objectives for each unit so that both the student and the tutor know exactly what has to be achieved.

3   Counselling and guidance are generally more easily available and relevant than in teacher-centred courses. This not only emphasizes the changed role of the tutor but also his importance in the student-centred approach. It also means that feedback can be regular and positive, encouraging and motivating the student.

4   Access to learning materials should be better than is normally the case for teacher-centred courses. Since well prepared and evaluated learning materials are an essential feature, the acquisition of knowledge is less dependent on the quality of individual teachers. There is also more opportunity for a variety of different media to be used within individualized learning units. Much of this material is produced for individualized and interactive use, involving the student in active participation and response. Many students find such a multi-media approach stimulating and motivating.

Disadvantages of the student-centred approach
The disadvantages may be summarized as:

1   *The active role of the student:* it may appear strange to describe this as a disadvantage. While it is one of the main reasons for developing a student-centred approach, one must not forget that it demands a higher degree of motivation and commitment on the part of the individual student. In teacher/institution-centred courses the student may adopt a much more passive role and still get by.

2   *The break with 'traditional' teaching:* in most cases this approach will be quite a different educational experience. Consequently, some of even the most motivated students may find it difficult, perhaps impossible, to adapt. The need to build in adequate student preparation for the student-centred approach must never be forgotten. It does mean more learning skills training and counselling at the beginning of the course.

3   *Time and cost of setting up the system:* open learning is not cheap, as the experience of the Open University has shown. The right administrative back-up and services are required. Learning resources facilities will be needed, some of which may have to be provided off campus. Others, such as laboratories and reference libraries, may need to be provided by the host institution at unsociable hours. Finally, although there may be less face-to-face class teaching, the academic staff will need to put in a tremendous amount of time and effort and this is extremely expensive. If the institution is running mainly teacher-centred courses then the promoters of open learning will have an uphill task to secure the finance and resources ncessary to make their efforts successful.

Student-centred learning in higher and further education today
The application of education technology should favour a move
towards more student-centred, open learning. The pace of technological change in the field of communications is continually providing
opportunities for individuals not only to acquire knowledge in
different ways but also to interact with it. Social, commercial and
industrial developments point up the need for more flexible educational patterns to prepare individuals for life and to enable them to
readjust to continually changing needs.

There are signs of initiatives: the Open Tech programme and, most
recently, the Open College. In some ways it would seem to be the
moment when we are poised for radical change and development in
higher and further education. Yet who can be confident that such
change will take place and, if it does, will it be directed towards
educational objectives and led by forward-looking educationalists
prepared to innovate?

There are problems, such as the following:

1 *Finance:* we have said that open learning is expensive, requiring
considerable investment to set up effective systems. In the present
situation of contraction it is difficult to see where the extra investment
is to come from. There could be a few eye-catching prestige projects,
but general availability of additional funds in colleges is unlikely to be
forthcoming.

2 *Other hands on the tiller:* the signs from government suggest
that an emphasis on vocational training may be linked with
commerce and industry having considerably increased influence.
There are clear hints in the government's Green Paper on higher
education which have been reinforced by the recent White Paper.
(Cmd. 114). We have already seen the impact of the Manpower
Services Commission on further education and developments such as
the Open College have the potential for real development. This may
not necessarily be a less innovative approach to learning. Some of the
study programmes, particularly in skills acquisition, may be well
suited to a student-orientated, interactive approach. For example
Anthony Steele,[5] Training Officer at the National Computing Centre,
writing recently on interactive video in education has the viewpoint of
'a computer person who has spent the last eight years producing
learning resources for use in industrial training and in further and
higher education'. Much benefit can come from such involvement
provided that the educational objectives of the courses are enhanced
and made relevant to contemporary needs. They must not be

submerged by short-term financial or industrial requirements.

3 *Educational conservatism:* perhaps the greatest barrier to change in a professional area of activity is the members of that profession. A profession exists to maintain and develop proper standards. It also implicitly or explicitly protects the interests of its members. In the previous paragraph we sounded a note of warning about the motives of others, be they politicians or representatives of trade and industry, when they become involved with education. An even greater threat to change and development exists from within our colleges. The natural professional conservatism of most lecturers is intensified by the present low morale and lack of confidence in what is frequently perceived to be the current government policy and attitude towards higher and further education.

Given a supportive and expanding higher and further education sector, there might just be the chance of a significant shift in lecturers' attitudes. There might be a sufficient number of enthusiastic, motivated individuals who would be prepared to appraise their own professional role in the light of the changing needs and opportunities offered by developments in communication technology. This could be the spearhead of a move towards more open learning systems leading to radical course development and an increase in real staff development. However, in times of cutback and retrenchment the natural tendency is to defend the status quo.

Perhaps the best hope lies in the developing information technologies. The truly interactive nature of computing; the development of interactive video and the ability to harness telecommunications to information transfer offer opportunities for individualized learning that were beyond our expectations a few years previously. If the potential of these developments to make a real increase in the quality of learning is recognized then at last there may be a serious attempt to shift the balance from teacher to learner.

Educational technology and college libraries

The significance of educational technology for college libraries should be readily apparent from the foregoing paragraphs. The definitions of educational technology and the debate about teacher and student-centred learning requires the librarian to define the library's contribution to the learning process. It reminds him that the library is both a facility and a mechanism for change.

Libraries have traditionally been seen as a support service for teaching. Students armed with reading lists descend upon the stock competing for copies of the texts specified on reading lists while 95%

of the collection remains relatively little used. In this situation the library is almost exclusively a reservoir of materials that reinforce lectures and provide the information on which written assignments can be based. In a teacher-centred course this 'fixes' the role of the library. It also determines the relationship between the teacher and the librarian. The move towards more student-centred, open learning requires a redefinition of roles. The significance of the library as a central part of the learning strategy cannot be ignored. It will demand considerable reappraisal of the library's role, what it provides, the services it offers and, perhaps most importantly, the attitude of its staff.

Later in the book we shall be considering the 'identity' of the college librarian. One of the ways in which this can be established is through an understanding of this wider concept of educational technology. This is not meant to imply that all librarians must have detailed knowledge of and experience in teaching and course design, desirable as that may seem in theory. Some college librarians who have previously been teachers may already have such experience.

We suggest that all librarians should try to understand and appreciate the nature and purpose of educational technology. This will enable them to:

- Acquire some understanding of learning situations and course design and adopt a more positive and informed approach when relating the potential of the library service to course needs.
- Engage in a positive dialogue with the educational technologist(s) in the college to their mutual benefit.
- Use the approaches of educational technology to help them develop their own management appraisal techniques and evaluate the performance of their systems.

References

1 Latcham, J. and Cuthbert, R., 'A systems approach to college management, *Coombe Lodge Report,* FESC, 11, (14), 1979, 589-93.
2 Percival, F. and Ellington, H., *A handbook of educational technology,* Kogan Page, 1984.
3 op. cit. 2.
4 op. cit. 2.
5 Steele, A., 'Interactive video in education: a trainer's view', *Learning Resources Journal,* 1, (2), LRDG, 1985, 4-8. Reprinted by permission of The National Computing Centre Ltd.

Chapter 5   The college library: a client-centred system

The library as a system

In the section on college management we looked at the college as a system. This involved three main aspects: inputs, outputs and the process. Added to that were the important mechanisms of a monitoring device and information feedback. The library is also a system in its own right; we must consider it as a system and also as a sub-system in relation to the macro system, the college.

Figure 5.1 applies the preliminary systems model for an enterprise (Figure 3.1) to the college library. It shows institutional requirement and client demand and the way the system responds to satisfy them. In so doing it demonstrates the pivotal position that the library holds between teacher-centred courses and the more individual, student-centred approach. In Chapter 4 on educational technology and educational objectives we said of the student-centred approach to learning, 'it is designed to meet the needs of the individual rather than the requirements of the institution'. Both of these approaches meet in the library.

The purpose of this chapter is to consider the library in terms of its clients. Earlier we asked 'Who are the college's customers?' Directly or indirectly the groups we identified then will make their input into the library. The responsibility of the library is to balance institutional requirement with individual need. They should have a large common element but they will not be identical. In some cases they will diverge, perhaps even become conflicting. This leads to stress and tension within the system and calls for managerial skills and leadership to resolve the situation.

The library system diagram shows a thread which runs through input, process and output that is client-centred. Input covers the demands of employers and clients (not identical or even complementary). Processes start with the assessment of client need in library terms and are followed by those activities which are necessary to satisfy that need. The performance outputs continue to demonstrate

Figure 5.1 The library as a system

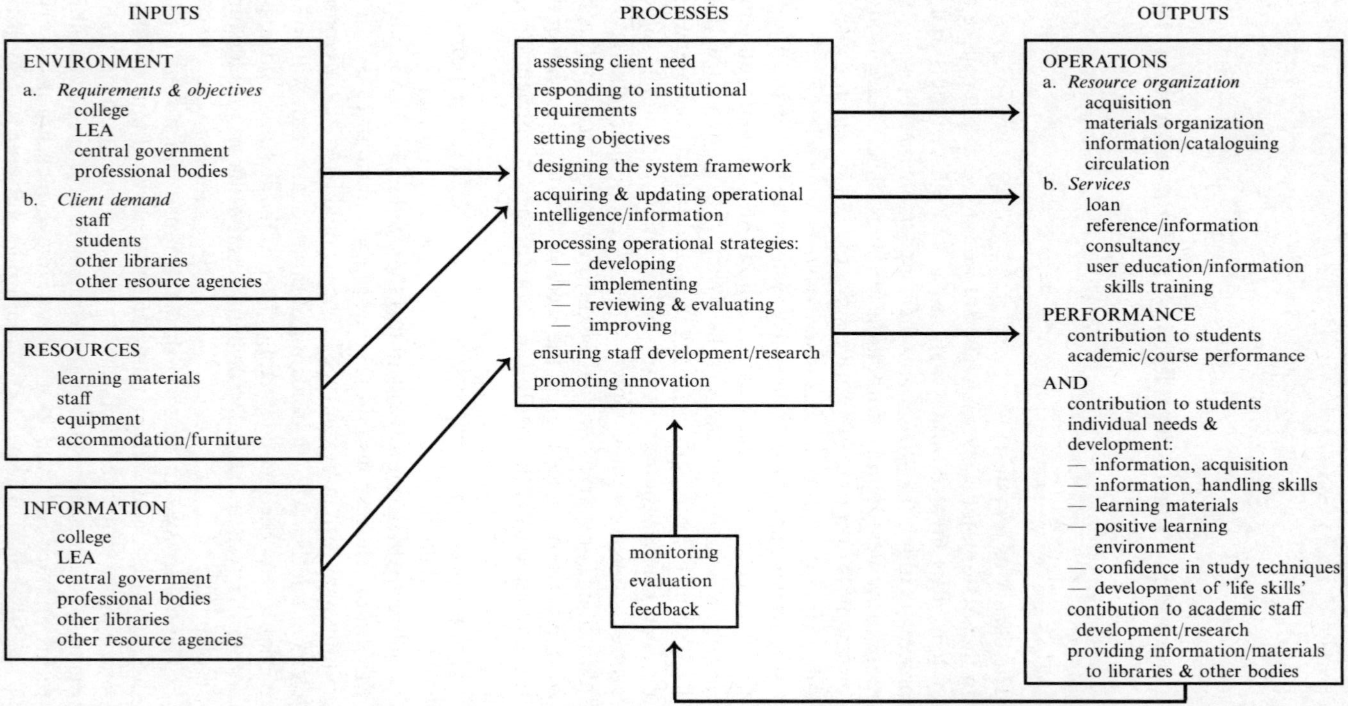

INPUTS

ENVIRONMENT
a. *Requirements & objectives*
   college
   LEA
   central government
   professional bodies
b. *Client demand*
   staff
   students
   other libraries
   other resource agencies

RESOURCES
   learning materials
   staff
   equipment
   accommodation/furniture

INFORMATION
   college
   LEA
   central government
   professional bodies
   other libraries
   other resource agencies

PROCESSES

assessing client need
responding to institutional
   requirements
setting objectives
designing the system framework
acquiring & updating operational
   intelligence/information
processing operational strategies:
   — developing
   — implementing
   — reviewing & evaluating
   — improving
ensuring staff development/research
promoting innovation

monitoring
evaluation
feedback

OUTPUTS

OPERATIONS
a. *Resource organization*
   acquisition
   materials organization
   information/cataloguing
   circulation
b. *Services*
   loan
   reference/information
   consultancy
   user education/information
      skills training

PERFORMANCE
   contribution to students
   academic/course performance

AND
   contribution to students
   individual needs &
   development:
   — information, acquisition
   — information, handling skills
   — learning materials
   — positive learning
      environment
   — confidence in study techniques
   — development of 'life skills'
   contribution to academic staff
      development/research
   providing information/materials
      to libraries & other bodies

both the college requirement of the students in course terms and their individual needs.

Into the first category comes learning materials used, information needs satisfied. Only incidentally would the library have contributed to the learning process and this could not be identified separately. The students would go on to complete their course assessment; the contribution the library made would be reflected in this. The second category where the library satisfies the client in his or her own right, will include those skills that are acquired in the handling of information as a result of consultation between client and librarian. It is cumulative, leading to self-confidence on the part of the client and can lead to a demonstrable increase in the ability to undertake and profit by individualized learning. It is an asset which, once acquired, can be used and further developed in different contexts throughout one's career.

The means of achieving this in terms of resource and information input, systems organization and materials deployment are important but they must follow and respond to the identified client needs. Two other considerations are important:

1   Human resources are the most important resource; this is well recognized among college teaching staff but it is easy to think of the library as a collection of materials and forget the human element. Staff development for library staff is absolutely crucial.

2   The system needs to be evaluated. This requires self-analysis but it also depends on feedback. Those who have experienced the library 'process' should have views on the quality and success of the 'output'. These views need to be incorporated into the evaluation if it is not to become an exercise in navel gazing. It is relatively easy to evaluate the efficiency of technical processes and to make assumptions about client need with the attendant danger that these assumptions reflect the kind of library service you want to provide rather than true client demand.

Because of the nature and purpose of a college library in the 1980s our perspectives must be kept in balance. We have considered the phenomena of contraction and uncertainty in colleges. One problem that can arise as a result of trying to formulate objectives is to think only in the short term. If change is the only constant then 'flexibility' must be the guiding principle. Yet what is flexibility? It is perfectly acceptable as an approach within a determined and consistent plan but an admission of failure if it becomes an alternative to planning.

The nature of a library is two-fold. It is both an agent for change and a conserving and coordinating force. In an information-rich society it will be the largest organized and accessible bank of information and ideas within the college and relevant to its needs. It does not merely support teaching: it can help to extend the range and quality of that teaching and encourage curriculum change. It is a major agency for individualized learning. Yet it can only realize those goals if there is consistent long-term planning and steady progress towards achieving objectives.

It is important when emphasizing demand and client need to bear this in mind. Responding on an ad hoc basis to all feedback is neither desirable nor sensible. The well managed library will have its long-term plan which is reviewed regularly. This will include provision for major developments *and* the opportunity to modify these and include other changes which are deemed necessary. Two words of warning. First, demand and client need should influence long-term planning positively and not inhibit it. Second, care must be taken to ensure that one responds to demand and perceived client need in a constructive and systematic way. Ad hoc responses to every demand that comes from staff and students could fray the edges of the service and perhaps damage it in the long term. How the librarian resolves this is a measure of the quality of his management.

What is being attempted is a library system that is highly relevant to the college system. Constant reviewing is essential because of the fluid nature of the desired goal. Educational philosophy and practice are constantly changing and the response of the educational librarian must change with it. We must give full weight to the impact of the IT revolution which has pushed through some of the attitudinal barriers. It has been the catalyst for a rethinking of long-held positions and has prompted new approaches to many previously accepted ideas. The fact that this revolution has already been with us for more than a decade and we do not appear to have grasped its significance fully is salutory. We tend to blame the political, social and economic climate and, while this may be justifiable to some extent, some of the difficulties lie with our own professional attitudes. If college librarians are to hold a credible position in the future, and college libraries are not to become an anachronism, we must face these issues positively and turn them to our advantage. McGlothlin[1] addressing the AALS conference in 1972 said:

> Unless we have vision we can have no sense of direction. Unless we have vision we cannot choose people to work or programs to undertake . . . the vision of a profession whose members have accepted their responsibility to increase professional competence at the rate and to the extent that the

dizzying changes of the world around them now require.

Moving on from this to more recent works on college librarianship which attempt to review and advise on desirable objectives and practice, e.g. McElroy,[2] Library Association,[3] NATFHE,[4] one is struck by how long we have been advised about the need for greater involvement in the wider environment in which our work is set and the adoption of a more proactive role. It would be unjust to suggest that there has not been considerable progress and a much improved library and librarian's image in many institutions, but there are still too many examples of college librarianship 'old style'.

Ignoring the client

There has been a tendency in the past to set up the sort of structure that satisfies the librarian's concept of an ordered library system even if it confuses rather than assists the client. It is easier to achieve this than to meet the clients' needs since these are variable and not as easy to identify. Failure to attempt the exercise must mean loss of relevance.

> *Stevenson:*[5] the revolution in user education, when it comes, will be less concerned with new methods and more with realistic and empathetic relationships between librarian and student and a clearer perception of their mutual purpose.

> *Jones:*[6] Ends in librarianship are inherently difficult to define, and there is a tendency to improve upon means the better to serve ends which remain largely unexamined. . . . Librarianship is traditionally means-centred or techniques-centred or, at least, materials-centred as opposed to being user-centred or aims-centred . . . the library manager is constantly faced with the problem of goal displacement, that is the tendency to lose sight of aims and purpose and to see means as ends in themselves.

> *Fletcher:*[7] The professionalism of our libraries should be rooted not in the ownership of resources, but in the objectives of our institutions . . . a college library is not merely an added amenity, but can become a central learning resource centre fully integrated into the college's teaching/learning function.

How do we make the library more client-centred?

Examining the college library in more detail with a view to achieving this state of real relevance to our clientele, what mechanisms are at our disposal to aid our planning?

Returning to the diagram (Figure 5.1) of the library as a system, the significance of starting with 'inputs' in section one and with requirements and objectives and client demand at the top of the list is now made plain, but not therefore, as will be demonstrated, simple! The diagrammatic representation of the system implies a tidy structure with one aspect following another. In practice this is of course not the case. The following paragraphs attempt to demonstrate the interrelationships of inputs, processes and outputs. We need to:

- Assess the information needs of students, staff and management.
- Negotiate for the necessary resources within the constraints and the context of the college system.
- Process these in cost-effective ways to achieve relevant and successful outputs.
- Evaluate and monitor these operations.

If this is to lead to an improved system it must be on-going, needing continual modification to respond to the dynamic environment within which it operates.

Assessing needs: ordering priorities
Systematic market research is necessary to identify those demands for services which are regarded as essential. Immediately we are into the area of subjectivity and value judgements. It is important to make the fullest possible review and order priorities against well thought out and justified criteria. Assessing demands is important for the reasons already stated but also because users' expectations, whether staff or student, tend to be low if not stimulated by a demonstration of library potential. In some areas of operation where students and perhaps teaching staff are not naturally library-orientated, this can mean identifying potential rather than actual demands. This will entail making potential library clients aware of the library's possible benefits to them. One has the difficult task of anticipating and stimulating demand.

Information gathering via committee structures
It is essential that professional library staff participate fully in college committees and working parties. This is important for the library's proper involvement with the college system. Librarians should make inputs at the various levels of the committee structures, i.e. user groups, curriculum development boards, course validation/approval working parties.

The librarian's potential contribution to this aspect of the college's work can be underestimated both by the librarian as well as other academic staff. Information about the implications for library provision in connection with new or modified courses is an obvious area but there are others. In meetings concerned with critical course evaluation and appraisal the librarian's contribution can have the added benefit of being more general and less partial. With moves towards student-centred and open learning the librarian can often have a particular expertise to offer in the areas of course design and curriculum development (see Percival[8]).

In addition to closer involvement with college committees, some members of the library staff will also find themselves involved in liaison exercises outside the college – with other library and resources agencies – building up a knowledge of the complementary resources available within the area or subject field, goodwill and mutual cooperation.

These exercises require the investment of a good proportion of staff time – a commodity which is in short supply. But the danger of sacrificing this long-term planning requirement to the short-term daily organizational needs of the service must be avoided. It is necessary, of course, to invest time in the various in-house materials-related processes (acquisition, organization, development) known in some libraries under the umbrella term, technical services. On a day-to-day basis these operations are very time-consuming, but if they take up all the librarian's time one can soon experience goal displacement and areas of irrelevance in the service. Ask yourself whether this is happening in your system and, if it is, look at the ways available to you to start correcting it.

Answers may lie in the need for refining, streamlining, or possibly mechanizing, some of the routines. It may be that you are genuinely short of staff, in which case taking time off from cataloguing the backlog or whatever the current bottleneck, to prepare and present a well argued case in the appropriate committees together with judicious lobbying for support could be of infinitely more value in the longer term than any catching up you might achieve in the routines for the short term. This argument applies equally to time invested in planning and executing staff development programmes – time-consuming exercises in the short term but valuable investment in one of the library's most important resources in the long term.

Management/employer relationships: getting resources and ordering priorities

While considering the librarian's relationship with the college structure a comment on the relationship with the college management is apposite. The principal and senior management may be 'users' in the general sense of the term, they may also make specific demands on the library, using it as part of the college's information system.

For the librarian the most usual and important role of management is as controller operating the library in the light of the various directives, restraints, constraints imposed by the system. Here the role is the delicate one of managing the politics of the system – making one's case for resources (revenue, capital, equipment, accommodation, staff) for the library service within the limits set by the paymasters, attempting to set the needs of the library in the context of the whole college budget, being realistic and objective in arguing the case and knowing how to apply appropriate checks and balances when other departmental managers are being less so. This may be a relatively new role for the librarian and one with which he is not readily familiar. In many cases he may have some catching up to do as far as operating with other heads of department and senior management staff is concerned.

Davinson[9] has a note of warning for us: 'Whilst many librarians have thriven mightily others have been bewildered and upset by the heat of the academic kitchen, where heads of departments fight each other hard for the resources they want.'

Note: This aspect is dealt with in more detail elsewhere – see Chapter 9, 'Thoughts about college librarians', and Chapter 8, 'Librarians and learning resources'.

Relations with 'the employer', which still usually means the local education authority, and with government/government agencies (which may be via the National Advisory Body and/or in many colleges the Manpower Services Commission and its various initiatives) will often be at one remove, i.e. the librarian will not be negotiating directly with these bodies and their representatives but will be reacting to their directives as received and interpreted via the college management. (The librarian should have a voice via ex-officio representation on the academic board to make a contribution when appropriate to the interpretation by management of relevant government/employer directives). It is important that the librarian keeps himself well informed and up-to-date with developments and current thinking of these bodies in order to grasp the significance of any White/Green Papers, policy changes, political pressures.

Relationships with local employers

It must be borne in mind that employer relationships have another meaning in the college context, namely the students' employers or potential employers and their demands indirectly as clients.

These will include:

- The perception of the in-service course organizer.
- The director of a local business or firm wanting a specific short course provided.
- The demands of a particular industry in terms of a relevant qualification.

The needs of this last group will often be expressed in part at least through the qualification- awarding, examination, validating bodies.

The librarian should aim to develop good relations with the college's industrial liaison officer, where this post exists. An information input from the library into consultancy work either through the industrial liaison officer or other channels existing in the college can help make this a two way process so that all parties benefit. This is very often a neglected area in college library work and there is considerable scope to increase the awareness of college consultants about the library's potential. In doing this one can demonstrate the library's value in a much more positive way.

Assessing needs: the contribution of validating bodies

It is important to emphasize the value to the library of the inputs of validating bodies. The time spent on work in preparation for submissions can cause frustration but the positive benefits must always be kept in mind. Davinson:[10] 'The validating bodies can supply the basic tools but it is up to the librarians to use them.'

The body which comes first to mind is the Council for National Academic Awards (CNAA). College librarians involved in the early days of CNAA validation often found that an institutional review or a course validation suddenly afforded them attention and support that they had been unable to attract previously. Members of academic staff responsible for library materials provision in relevant subject areas who had previously had little time for the library were to be found requesting items, arguing for more library funding and being generally more supportive of the service – the librarian had allies in the most unexpected quarters! In some cases the pressures were applied even more widely, the local authority being persuaded to agree library extensions, staffing increases and expenditure on resources in considerably increased measure rather than have validation refused or withdrawn.

In the prevailing economic climate this kind of upgrading exercise is on a more modest scale and with the gradual introduction of self-validation in colleges we may see a further change of emphasis. Though the CNAA has never agreed to colleges quoting actual required standards of library provision in precisely quantified terms and has deliberately never produced 'standards' of its own, there is no doubt that the requirement for colleges to prepare detailed reports and critical evaluations of their systems, including detailed reviews of learning resources provision and management, has entailed a very valuable series of exercises for many colleges demanding a level of thinking and discipline that many would otherwise never have found the time to undertake. There is little doubt that colleges, and their libraries, have benefited greatly from this type of exercise even though on some occasions there has been an expenditure of time and effort which seemed out of proportion to the end result. With the introduction of self-accreditation, and eventually credit transfer, perhaps a better balance between the time invested and the 'return' to the college will be achieved.

CNAA is not the only validating body with which colleges are involved of course but it has been the body creating most impact, and this is particularly true in library terms. This is partly because, having a dual role, i.e. institutional reviewing and course validation as two separate undertakings, CNAA review panels and visiting consultants are *genuinely* concerned with and *do* closely monitor learning resources provision in the institutions they visit. In the case of so many other organizations, however, consideration of library and learning resources provision has been very much a token gesture rather than a serious exercise. Examples which come to mind from personal experience are BTEC and its predecessors, Central Council for Education and Training in Social Work, Chartered Institution of Building Services.

All these bodies, in their documentation relating to syllabus content and to assessment, as well as in submissions for course approval, make reference to library materials and facilities for individual study. In practice, however, there has been, in the authors' experience at least, little on-site evaluation of these facilities by visiting validating officers.

Following a course review visit other pressures can arise. Experiences remembered are of teaching staff arriving in the library after receiving critical reports from visiting course HMIs or examining body reviewers and subjecting the librarian to considerable pressure to persuade him, on an ad hoc basis, to make good the deficiencies that have been highlighted in time for the next visit. The librarian then has to deploy a good measure of tact, remembering that numerous requests made to the department for booklists have previously fallen on deaf ears. In some cases allocations remained partially unspent at the end of the financial year because the lecturers concerned could not find time to submit request lists.

It is pleasing to note that this state of affairs is beginning to change. Documentation sent out by the English National Board for Nursing, for example, to colleges applying for approval for courses in nursing, midwifery and health visiting, includes detailed requests for information on library and learning resources. This board recently took over functions from the former statutory and training bodies and established a working group to rationalize the extant diverse procedures. A single procedure appropriate to each of the professional groups was accepted in principle by the Board in March 1985. Their *Guidelines*[11] which accompany an application to proceed with the development of a course submission:

1 List 'librarian services' as one of five categories under the 'staff' heading and state 'the number of library staff and their qualifications should be given'.

2 In a section devoted to teaching accommodation and learning resources state: 'There must be adequate and up-to-date library services and other learning resources and adequate means of making these available to units away from the main centre. The description of the library services available should include the aim of services, accommodation, physical resources, information resources and reader services together with funding arrangements.'

3 In the section 'course content, structure and organisation', state: 'learning resources should be identified and how they will be used'.

A head of learning resources in a college of higher education offering ENB courses tells us that he has found this documented approach and subsequent discussions with ENB visitors most helpful.

Visits by HMIs to the college can help to give weight to the library's case for improved resources and their reports, now that they are published, can provide useful guidelines to the librarian in making provision relevant to courses.

Colleges that are preparing to offer themselves as support centres for the Open College will find themselves with exacting conditions to fulfil – Burton and Mauger:[12] 'A "licence" to provide these student support services will only be granted by Open College once the services are perceived as being of high quality and readily available'. But as a result of this development, they are presented with an opportunity for radical self-examination – Burton and Mauger:[13] 'The challenges to learning resources are fundamental. The implications go beyond the Open College. It may well lead us to examine how we deliver learning to *all* our students'.

So, improvements are happening in some colleges for some subject areas but need to happen in them all. If you are not satisfied with the state of affairs in your college, rather than burn up energy getting exasperated with the existing situation try to turn it positively to your advantage. Course board and curriculum development committee meetings, user group discussions, both formal and informal, can be used to good effect to anticipate validation requirements which can become cooperative and more orderly exercises. An example from personal experience was the successful negotiation of a specific section, "Library Resources Implications" on a newly designed course approval form, and the subsequent following-up by the noting of new courses as they were submitted on the rolling plan for the academic board, and by approaching staff concerned for discussions in the early stages.

Practical approaches of this nature must be identifiable within your system which can be used for improving cooperation and leading to purposeful stock building. This in turn can lead to a more relevant approach to user education, demonstrating that time taken from tightly packed syllabuses and timetables for this purpose can be cost effective, in effect often saving time and having longer-term benefits as a bonus.

A planned approach to those areas of library management which have an obvious and direct bearing on the teaching and student body, involving the clientele at an early stage and in an organized way in discussions and developments, all help towards a more relevant provision and can do a great deal for the librarian's credibility and status within the college. Many hard-pressed colleagues working in underdeveloped systems are going to protest that they have not got the staff or time to get involved in these exercises in relationships and user education. The response must be that college librarians *cannot afford not to get involved* in them if the relevance we are striving for is to be achieved. We reiterate our earlier advice on the ordering of priorities and/or the improving of the 'workforce'.

Assessing needs: requirements identified by ways other than formal validation
Discussions of the validation procedure have been concerned primarily with relations with academic staff though there is a place on

70

some committees for student opinion and this should certainly be included as part of course monitoring and feedback.

Both staff and students use and relate to the library on many occasions for purposes which have no direct connection with validation procedures. These need to be identified and catered for just as carefully, though the process will not be so straightforward since these operations do not always fit into a neat pattern as, for example, CNAA review documentation or a BTEC National Certificate in business studies, or a CCETSWA Certificate of Qualification in social work course submission.

Many of these staff and student needs arise either as a direct or indirect outcome of educational developments currently taking place. These developments have very specific inferences for college libraries affecting parts of the system quite radically, for example, in staff recruitment, staff development, accommodation requirements, cooperation with other departments.

In an attempt to come to terms with these changes and their implications we identify some of the issues (readers will undoubtedly be able to add some of their own) and comment upon their effects on the system.

Changes in the college clientele

The term 'colleges' covers a wide range of institutions with a great variety of subjects and levels of courses. The clientele across both AFE and NAFE is constantly changing but this is particularly so in those colleges which have a large proporton of NAFE. This is due in large measure to the economic climate and the employment situation that currently obtains. Many of these changes have been referred to in an earlier chapter in general college terms and they have a significance for library and learning resource centre planning. Raddon:[14] 'Resources provision must be integrated to and totally supportive of educational change. This in turn implies change and flexibility within the profession to carry out this crucial role.'

The establishment of the Manpower Services Commission by the Department of Trade and Industry with its many initiatives to alleviate the rapidly rising unemployment figures throughout the 1980s, and the competitive/collaborative schemes of the Department of Education and Science to counteract increasing encroachment of the DTI in education, have been responsible for a quite substantial change in the college profile and teaching methods of many institutions. Related to this, debates on the inadequacy of preparation for work and the evolvement of such programmes as CPVE and

71

TVEI have led to major re-thinking about the provision for the 16 to 18 age group which has brought schools and colleges into closer contact with one another. In some instances the influence of this debate and the prevailing local economic circumstances have had far reaching effects resulting in total restructuring of organizations into tertiary institutions. Much of this is still in the formative stages and should offer the chance for librarians along with other learning resource professionals to be involved in policy and planning discussions enabling them to influence the nature of resource provision and its management. Leach:[15]

> Where a multiple tertiary college system, or tertiary education system is being formed then typically the LEA is very proactive regarding the respective roles of the new colleges; philosophy, planning, distribution of courses, marketing, student admissions policies, college structures and gradings of staff, are all subjected to policy formulation at the LEA level. Elected members, officers, advisers, advisory teachers, college senior staff and authority-wide union representatives are all involved in the process.
>
> Financial resources are focused on the planned change, and inter-institutional cooperation between the newly planned colleges becomes an imperative. The client view, whether it be student, employer or other agencies working with the college system, can be quite difficult to get through in the planning stage.
>
> It is in this scenario that the learning resources professionals in a reorganizing situation have to make their influence felt. It means mobilizing and organizing, thinking and planning, in order to make constructive proposals soon enough at the right level at the right time.

Note: A substantial quote is given here but the whole article is very pertinent and commended to the reader.

MSC/DES initiatives in the mature sector have also had their influences, whether institutions have become involved for sound educational reasons or have been tempted by the prospect of additional funding.

The DES Pickup[16] programme is a prime example of this with its consortia, which now number over twenty and which are aimed at adult training, retraining and updating. Other Pickup initiatives include cooperation with bodies other than colleges – for example the cooperative projects with the Institute of Personnel Management – 'A partnership in Learning'[17] and the Health Pickup Project.[18]

Another example is the Open Tech[19] programme which by May 1987 had over 140 current projects some of which are college-based.

Alternative funding for college courses is becoming more widespread. With the squeezing of funds from traditional sources and pressures from bodies like the Audit Commission for colleges to be more closely scrutinized for cost-effective performance, and for rationalization across the country, this tendency must grow. Salmon[20] examines this in some detail and indicates some of its effects on college clientele and on teaching and learning patterns.

> The future for public sector spending depending less and less on full-time students, will require considerable flexibility in course provision, increased access for students with scope for home-based and intermittent study leading to transferable credit accumulation and modular qualifications. Mixed-grade groups of students, reinforced by distance learning using mass-market media, shorter intensive foundation courses, increased use of packaged material and less insistence on re-inventing the wheel by teachers determined to have their own 'ego trip' – all these phenomena will cause radical changes in teaching and learning methods. Student-centred learning and employer involvement in curriculum delivery will increase demands for staff appraisal.

Changes in teaching and learning patterns
Student-centred learning
The desire to shift the emphasis from class-taught to more student-centred learning is not new. (*Note:* Chapter 4 on 'Educational technology and educational objectives' examines teacher-centred and student-centred learning in more detail.)

It is now many years since observations were first made of too much time spent in the classroom with teachers giving out their distilled wisdom, and of a need to formulate learning programmes which involved students more in doing, researching and discovery. Gradually, evidence of this process taking place is to be seen in college curricula and syllabuses. If students are not to be ensconced in formal classrooms, where are the alternative places they will learn? The library or resources centre will rank high among the alternatives, much assignment and project work will be seen to be library-orientated.

Open learning
Project and assignment work may be undertaken in groups or singly but another development – flexible, distance, open or individualized learning – is concerned with the structuring of programmes tailored to individual needs and in which timing is placed very much in the hands of the learner rather than, as in the traditional patterns, dictated by the teachers and course organizers. FEU:[21] 'The adaptation of available learning opportunities to meet the needs of the

learner in a way that optimizes the autonomy of the learner as well as the effectiveness of the process of learning.'

The pioneers in this field (in the mid 1970s), apart from the very particular case of the Open University, are probably the Open College at Nelson and Colne which 'provides a route for mature students with no formal educational qualifications to go on to further and higher education' (Maltby[22]) and the Flexistudy system at Barnet College 'which combines the home study of correspondence material with tutorial contact (and which) meets the needs of students who are unable or unwilling to attend full or part-time courses offered in the conventional mode'. (Adams[23]).

(Note: for other accounts on open learning see Adams, LRDG Bulletin no.4, April 1981; Birch and Latcham, 'Managing open learning', papers presented to a seminar Chorley College FESC; Fletcher, Coombe Lodge Report vol. 17, no. 3, 1984; FEU, *Flexible learning in action,* and *Flexible learning opportunities 1984* and *Flexible learning opportunities 1983* and *Implementing open learning in local authority institutions,* 1986; Percival *et al, Distance learning and evaluation,* Kogan Page, 1981; and Spencer, *Thinking about open learning systems,* CET, 1980.)

Competence-based learning
The Further Education Unit, another DES development founded in 1974 (though now operating independently as a limited company), has both commissioned and collaborated on studies that have significance as far as teaching and learning patterns are concerned. Reference has already been made to its flexible learning projects. *Towards a competence-based system*[24] starts from a common concern to raise standards of education and training to a level of understanding as opposed to time-serving. Competence is defined as 'the possession and development of sufficient skills, knowledge, appropriate attitudes and experience for successful performance in life roles'. Such a definition includes employment, maturity and responsibility in a variety of roles and it includes experience as an essential element:

> Our delivery systems in education and training tend to be unnecessarily polarized; between academic and vocational learning, between high- and low-level teaching, between 'real' work-based and 'abstract' classroom assignments. We have much to learn as professionals about how we can organize the acquisition of competence (in the way we now wish to define it) . . . by a wide range of learners. Teachers need to work together . . . in planning integrated approaches. . .

This has major implications for staff development, cooperation and user education programmes.

Continuing professional development
Continuing professional development: a learner-centred strategy[25] and *Learning from experience,*[26] 'are centred on the requirements of mid-career adults who wish to maintain or promote their professional standing'. Concentrating on the 'experience' element in the earlier definition of competence-based learning, specific cases in the field of engineering are described but it is maintained that 'the method is applicable wherever adult students need assistance in articulating and capitalizing on their experience in order to obtain a particular goal'. The second volume is a practical manual intended as a companion volume to the first:

> The main message of both volumes is that in provision of courses for the Continuing Professional Development of adults it is essential to recognize and exploit their store of experiential learning. Participative workshop sessions provide the supportive environment in which adults can develop both their abilities and their confidence. The successful implementation of such a strategy requires teaching staff to adopt a facilitative rather than a didactic role which may be unfamiliar to many teachers of a technical subject.

The strategy includes such matters as assessment of the tutor's own needs, building up and keeping current a data base of information, verification of data and assessing students' needs. This is yet another area where there are far-reaching implications for staff development, user education and resource provision.

Information technology
This development and how it affects the library service is so wide-ranging and impinges on so many aspects of the library operation that a whole chapter has been devoted to it (see Chapter 7). At this point we note briefly that:

1   Our clientele is becoming increasingly computer-literate and will have growing expectations of library services in this medium – whether in the form of facilitating aids, e.g. COM catalogues, desk-top published reading lists, library guides etc.; reference sources in the form of computerized data bases, e.g. Medlars, Blaise, Ecctis, Maris, Prestel; back-up copies of tutors' teaching packages or commercially produced educational software packages to supplement the other library media i.e. books, journals, audio-visual materials.

2 Automated library systems have given us a powerful management tool so far in advance of anything we ever had before, that stock control, evaluation of service, efficiency of processing both stock and readers' services can be undertaken to a degree of specificity and efficiency far in excess of anything we might have contemplated a decade ago.

3 The implementation of IT-led developments needs a very different approach – a new way of looking at documentation, storage, exploitation, user education, library lay-out; and at the same time, the existing system with the conventional materials has largely to be retained. This will undoubtedly bring problems but IT must be a part of our operation if we are going to be relevant in the next decade and problems must be approached positively. A balance must be struck, the clients' needs must be kept at the forefront of our planning, organization and management and the paraphernalia of IT must be seen for what it is – a tool, though a complex, sophisticated and powerful one to serve our ends. The librarian must neither 'hide his head in the sand' and pretend it isn't there nor must he become mesmerized with the new devices and let them become ends instead of means. Staff development programmes for library staffs have an important part to play in this area. *Education:*[27]

> The application of IT techniques to aid learning must enhance rather than diminish the role of teachers and educationists must seize the opportunities offered by IT, in order that the growth of alternative educational methods is moderated by sound educational principles and that educationists maintain the relevance of their own approach to education in a fast-changing world.

Effects of these recent developments on the college library system
Implications for staff development (both teaching staff and library personnel), user education, provision of resources and interdepartmental cooperation have already been referred to.

Dean's[28] recent survey of three selected LEAs to ascertain the impact of TVEI on school and college libraries is not very encouraging reading and shows one development where an opportunity for greater involvement has not been fully grasped. One is left with the feeling that this is not the only area.

Considerations of what kind of library environment is the most appropriate are brought sharply into focus; for example, students coming to the college via the TVEI, YTS, CPVE routes, return to study clients (whether from Pickup or CPD) are unlikely to be used to and may well be put off by a traditional 'academic' library ambience. Provision centred round IT outlets, cross-modular assignment or other group projects tend to create a more restless atmosphere which may conflict (if accommodation is restricted) with other library users involved in more intensive individual research activities. These developments lead to conflicting demands on accommodation.

Independent learners often have very particular needs not immediately attributable to data supply – Adams:[29]

> Anyone who has studied by correspondence will understand the loneliness of learning at a distance. Often the problems which arise have little to do with the difficulty of the academic content of the course, but rather with motivation, self-discipline, confidence, the application of study skills . . . the library staff, seen as independent and 'neutral' figures in a college, find themselves in the position of adopting a counselling role as well as assisting with information retrieval.
>
> As professional librarians we cannot turn our backs on a new vital development in education whatever our resource problems. There is a place . . . for a partnership of college librarians as well as tutors and learning materials providers in the Open Learning Federation. Should an open learning network be achieved, libraries will have a key role to play.[30]

Open College developments, though only at the formative stages at the time of writing, confirm these views. There are plans for countrywide student support centres. These will require a wide range of facilities, staffed for periods exceeding traditional college opening hours.

A more entrepreneurial approach to funding and course provision, cooperative ventures with other colleges, with industry and with other professional bodies may all involve teaching staff in materials production. Because of developments in the technology, production of learning materials is now easier but in many cases it is only likely to be cost-effective if undertaken collaboratively. Learning materials may be open learning packages, audio-visual, interactive video, other computerized packages and all have potential for creating new and increased demands for use of library resources if librarians and other resource professionals show themselves to be responsive and their collections relevant.

Closer cooperation with industry opens up library potential in areas such as selective dissemination of current information from technical sources (e.g. trade specifications, British and other standard specifications, patent literature, Anbar management abstracts) which in turn could lead to closer cooperation with other sources (e.g. public commercial and technical libraries, business school libraries).

Preparation of current awareness bulletins can be a speedier and more efficient operation if the 'new technology' is used effectively.

Evaluation

Jones:[31]

> Many systems which claim to measure cost-effectiveness focus on the cost side of the equation and pay scant regard to effectiveness in meaningful educational terms. Effectiveness is often seen as a simple body count regardless of the effect of the system on those bodies.

For the college library to operate effectively, there must be regular monitoring and evaluation of the resources and services. By doing this it is possble to test the success and relevance of the library system and to keep it abreast of changing needs arising from developments in other parts of the college.

The Audit Commission reports and subsequent commentary upon them have recently brought questions of cost-effectiveness sharply into focus. Reactions encountered in the college as a whole with regard to the validity of some of the commission's criteria for measurement apply to an even greater degree when attempts are made to evaluate the college library. Again we are faced with questions of how we define achievement and success for the client in library terms. What, for example, is the mark of an educated student? We have stressed the need for objectives to enable the organization to build up a relevant service and approach but it is neither easy to design objectives specific enough to have tangible meaning yet sufficiently wide for general application, nor is it easy to assess how far such objectives have been met. Problematic in any of the educational institutions within our remit, the task is even more difficult in those which are larger and more diverse.

There have been several studies on the evaluation of library services. Clark[32] looks at research methodology and evaluation specifically as it applies to user education. This account is additionally useful for its attempts to differentiate between formative, summative and illuminative evaluation and for the bibliography. Lancaster[33] is now something of a standard work but it is of limited value for our purpose since the objectives as defined in its early chapters are too vague and all-embracing:

> The objective of the library is to maximize the accessibility of these (bibliographic) resources to the user or to maximize the exposure of the user to the resources. In addition, the library should be organized to minimize the amount of effort required to obtain access to needed

bibliographic materials, and to supply such materials as soon as possible when the need for them arises.

Lancaster's detailed service-by-service review and catalogue of existing studies for each aspect of service (i.e. catalogue use, reference services, library standards) is thorough and helpful in terms of quantitative evaluation but offers no real assistance with a qualitative approach in the ways needed by college librarians – though he does offer a thought provoking quotation from Meder:[34]

> Standards should be stated in terms of quality 'norms' and a description of excellence. Quantitative standards will not in the long run produce good libraries. The starting point for effective standards lies in the objectives of libraries themselves; to be valuable they must be directly related to the resources and objectives of the institution.

Wills and Oldman's[35] study is interesting since it is exclusively concerned with academic libraries and 'involved exploring the *interactions* between library type information systems and their receiving communities':

> The investigation has resulted in the conviction that methods have been devised and identified for measuring the differences between users' expectations of a library system and their experiences when in contact with that system . . . Such user orientation, rather than the traditional archival or product orientation, can normally lead to more effective management of resources. . . Librarians should see themselves as in the communication facilitation industry not the book supply industry.

Biggs[36] brings the subject right up to date and puts it very specifically in our context. Highlighting the administrative and political requirements, she looks at the need for cost benefit analysis in college libraries and, by comparing the approaches to the subject of Spriggs[37] and Donovan,[38] demonstrates how qualitative evaluation does not have to be sacrificed to quantitative, admitting however that 'unfortunately the kind of evidence required by the Audit Inspectorate is much easier to collect'. But, 'Librarians need both objective and subjective performance measures of their service'.

Allred[39] outlines some of the problems pinpointing the apparent conflict between the goals of the academic staff for teaching and those of librarians for student learning, the lack of clarity of goals or at least the high cost of negotiating them and the 'catch 22 situation' in that as use of the library increases the dissatisfaction factor rises, greater demands being made with increased expectations, so that use of library is not necessarily a good evaluation measure. It is, he says, more useful to understand the process – why people use the service:

'Mechanical measurement techniques have not helped to get at real use and value of the libraries or to analyse requirements. Profile evaluation is more effective than general statistics'.

Wilson[40] describing experiences, including the presentation of a dissertation, attempting an evaluation of the library service at Suffolk College of Higher and Further Education concluded:

> That in order to maximize its contribution to college objectives the library must be a dynamic organization capable of satisfying a range of changing needs rather than meeting theoretical quantitative criteria.
>
> Thus the conclusions and recommendations of this dissertation (Flatt[41]) are more concerned with organizational matters than the number of books, physical area or similar statistical measurements.

The dissertation is interesting as it was researched by a senior lecturer in the department of business and secretarial studies at the college who is library representative for his department. It attempts therefore to look at the problem from a different perspective and claims less bias than assessments made by librarians.

Real attempts have been made to gain feedback from users and to assess relevance of the service in qualitative educational terms. The main impressions one gains from reading the results of the user surveys are:

- That collection of suitable data is a difficult exercise.
- That attitudes towards the library by users tends to be somewhat apathetic and expectations low.

However, the fact that the survey was undertaken in this way is a significant and healthy indicator. If the experience described at Suffolk is at all typical of user perceptions in general then librarians have much to do. Nevertheless significant observations are made in the conclusions section and are all the more interesting since they are made from a user's point of view:

> library evaluation tends to fall into the arena of academic politics and inter-professional argument . . . a new approach to library evaluation needs to be adopted which does not evaluate for evaluation's sake. The objective should be to assess the extent to which the college library contributes to institutional objectives and how well it uses the resources allocated to it in doing so. The evaluation criteria will be specific to the needs of each college and formulated by its own staff.

Having established the need for a greater measure of qualitative evaluation we arrive at the question – 'How is it to be done?' Biggs[42] in answer to the question she poses herself 'Who will do the evaluation?' gives an incomplete answer – it is impossible to do otherwise:

In some cases the librarian will decide that evaluation must be done by library staff on site. In many other cases the library staff will not have the knowledge of techniques or the staff or the time available. Much will depend upon the purpose of the evaluation, whether it is intended to be formative or summative, to answer a purely local need or one which could be of national relevance. Few librarians will as yet be trained in techniques such as drafting of attitude rating scales or illuminative evaluation whereas profiling or case studies may be the more familiar medium. There is a need therefore for national guidance and research . . . and interest of validating bodies such as CNAA and BTEC.

Chambers and Harrison[43] are working on an overall 'Framework' for the evaluation of library services, prompted by Davinson's[44] view that course validators do not have the background to allow them to make informed judgements on the adequacy of a college's library services.

Their survey is presented under four main headings: The college, The library within the college, Factual data about the college and Analytical/evaluative framework.

A 'flavour' of the approach may be appreciated from the following sample questions:

What means exist to facilitate communication between library and teaching staff outside the committee structure? How does the librarian contribute to the policy making bodies of the College? How is curriculum and course planning information fed back into the library system? Does the College/Library have any mechanisms to measure educational benefit?

Chambers[45] develops this in a separate article giving a useful up-to-date background survey. His analysis supports our own view that the system should be directed towards the client and his needs and that any evaluation should be attempting primarily to assess efficiency and effectiveness in terms of meeting educational objectives. He acknowledges that evaluation of this sort is a difficult task but suggests that

between them, librarian and college administration already have the majority of the statistical information required (and that) the additional effort of analysis, presentation and discussion allows any college to monitor its library's practices and procedures for efficiency and further to assess the effectiveness of its services in terms of how far they are achieving prestated objectives.

Referring to work done at Further Education Staff College conferences he illustrates the type of process required asking analytical questions about relationships with users, the nature of usage, use of library accommodation and library costs relative to college costs.

It is anticipated that this type of analysis will be featured fully in the next revision of the LA COFHE Guidelines for college library services.

There is considerable activity in this area of college librarianship at the moment. This has undoubtedly been prompted by the activities of the Audit Commission initially and although there was protest at the way in which the commission approached the subject, it has stimulated an exercise in self-examination among professionals which ought to prove very beneficial.

In our reference on p.137 (Chapter 8, 'Libraries and learning resources') we offer two practical suggestions, namely user group assessment and outside consultancy, and give the outline of an existing research project along the lines suggested by Biggs.

References

1   McGlothlin, W.J., 'Continuing education in the professions', *Journal of Education for Librarianship,* 13, (1), 1972, 3-16.
2   McElroy, A.R. (ed.), *College librarianship: the objectives and practice,* Library Association, 1984.
3   Library Association, *College libraries: guidelines for professional service and resource provision,* 3rd. edn, Library Association, 1982.
4   NATFHE, *College libraries: a policy statement,* NATFHE, 1982.
5   Stevenson, M.B., in Malley, I. (ed), 'Educating the user', papers given at a two-day conference, 16 and 17 November 1977, Library Association, 1979, 14.
6   Jones, K., 'Creative library management' in Shimmon, R., *A reader in library management,* Bingley, 1976, 49.
7   Fletcher, E., 'New curricula: educational implications and impact on learning-centred resources', *Coombe Lodge Report,* 17, (3), FESC, 1984, 80.
8   Percival, Dr. F., 'The role of learning resources (educational development) units in curriculum change and development', *Learning Resources Journal,* LRDG, 3, (2), 1987, 46-55.
9   Davinson, D., 'Validating and examining bodies and the college library', in McElroy, op. cit. 2, 54.
10   op. cit. 9.
11   English National Board for Nursing, Midwifery and Health Visiting, *Approval process for courses in nursing, midwifery and*

health visiting, Circular 1987/28/MAT, ENB, 1987.

12   Burton, H. and Mauger, S., 'The Open College and its support service requirements', *Learning Resources Journal,* LRDG, 1987, 3, (2), 56.

13   op. cit. 12, 65.

14   Raddon, R., 'Planning resources centres', *Coombe Lodge Report,* 17, (3), FESC, 1984, 95.

15   Leach, M., 'Tertiary reorganization: its implications for learning resources professionals', *Learning Resources Journal,* LRDG, 1987, 3, (1), 10.

16   Department of Education and Science, *Pickup in progress,* DES, 11, September 1986.

17   Institute of Personnel Management, *A partnership in learning,* DES/Pickup, September 1986.

18   Health Pickup, *DES press release,* 12 September, 1986, (234/86).

19   Open Tech Programme, 'Projects underway', *Supplement to Open Tech Programme News,* no 13, MSC, 1987.

20   Salmon, M., 'Towards 2000: speculations about the future of higher education', *Learning Resources Journal,* 3, (1), LRDG, 1987, 5.

21   Further Education Unit, 'Flexible learning opportunities', in *Flexible learning in action,* Project report, FEU, 1984, 3.

22   Maltby, P.R., 'The Open College student and the library', in City of London Polytechnic, *The part-time student in the library,* LLRS publishing, 1983, 95.

23   Adams, M., 'Flexistudy and the college library', in op. cit. 22, 91.

24   Further Education Unit, *Towards a competence-based system, an FEU view,* FEU, 1984.

25   Further Education Unit, *Continuing professional development: a learner-centred strategy,* FEU, 1986.

26   Further Education Unit, *Learning from experience,* an FEU/ Pickup Occasional paper, FEU, 1986, (v).

27   Hartles, R. 'Week by week', *Education,* 168, (16), 1986, 327.

28   Dean, M., 'Impact of TVEI on school and college libraries', *Education Libraries bulletin,* 29, (2), 1986, 27-36.

29   op. cit. 23, 91.

30   op. cit. 23, 93.

31   Jones, D., 'Efficient effectiveness in colleges: a practical approach', *Coombe Lodge Report,* 18, (3), FESC, 1985, 138.

32   Clark, D. *et al., The travelling workshops experiment in library user education,* British Library Research and Development report 5602, British Library, 1981, 7-17.

33   Lancaster, F.W., *The measurement and evaluation of library services,* Arlington, VA, Information Resources Press, 1977, 8. Reprinted by permission of the publisher.

34   Meder, E., 'Accrediting agencies and the standards', *Drexel Library Quarterly* 2, 1966, 213-19.

35   Wills, G. and Oldman, C., *The beneficial library: a methodological investigation to identify ways of measuring the benefits provided by libraries,* Cranfield Institute of Technology School of Management, BLR & D Report 5389, British Library, 1977, 3 and 45.

36   Biggs, D., 'The college library: a valued resource', *Education Libraries Bulletin,* 29, (3), 1986, 2-21.

37   Sprigg, J. 'Evaluation of library services' paper given at LA CoFHE/ELG joint annual study conference, Chester College of HE, 1-4 April 1985 (unpublished to date).

38   Donovan, K.G., *Learning resources in colleges: their organization and management,* CET, 1981.

39   Allred, J., 'Evaluation of library services' paper given at LA CoFHE/ELG joint annual study conference, Chester College of HE, 1-4 April 1985, and published in Lomas, T. (ed), *Management issues in academic libraries,* Rossendale, 1986, 22-31.

40   Wilson, R.T.M., 'The perennial problem of evaluation', *CoFHE bulletin,* 45, Autumn 1985, 4.

41   Flatt, D.E., *Evaluation of a college library: an investigation into the problems of evaluating college libraries,* A study presented as part requirement for the Diploma of Further Eduation, University of Leeds, April 1985.

42   op. cit. 36, 17.

43   Chambers, F. and Harrison, C., 'Evaluating library services', *CoFHE Bulletin,* 45, Autumn 1985, 1-3.

44   Davinson, D., 'Validating and examining bodies', in McElroy, A.E. (ed), op. cit. 2, 54.

45   Chambers, F., 'Evaluating the college library: is it worth it?', *Coombe Lodge Report,* 19, (9), FESC, 1987, 587-600.

Chapter 6   User education

Having attempted to identify client needs in order to build up the sources and services of the college library and having considered the question of evaluation, another major process of the system needs to be examined. This is the function which is generally referred to under the term 'user education'.

> User education has four aims: to enhance student learning, to encourage user independence, to widen the use of a range of library resources and to introduce the library and its staff to its users.
>
> Herring[1]

Libraries have operated some form of user education for a very long time. As far back as the mid-seventeenth century John Durie in his *Reformed Librarie Keeper* (1650) said 'the role of the librarian should be taken to include assistance or instruction in the proper use of the library's stock'.[2]

The range of programmes and the degree of acceptance of the concept varies tremendously from institution to institution.

'Despite the length of time it (i.e. library instruction) has been around it is still not widely accepted as a legitimate part of the librarian's work by many academic staff . . .' Cowley.[3] Malley[4] gives a useful survey of the current state of the art and contrasts the attitudes and approaches between polytechnic and college libraries drawing on findings in a survey of user education programmes organized by him as British Library Information Officer for User Education, Malley and Moys[5]. Clark[6] gives a useful review of the key writings on user education and on research methodology and evaluation.

Both Malley's and Clark's accounts indicate that there is a great deal of work to be done and that there are many constraints and problems – not least in the areas of resourcing, and staff resourcing in particular:

> Although all these surveys indicate an enormous increase in activity, they are also unanimous in agreeing that many major problems remained unsolved, that not enough was being done, that in some cases the wrong

things were being done and that there was a general need for a new more subtle approach.   Clark[7]

Despite all the discussing and experimenting there has been little progress towards a workable solution (or set of solutions), because it is actually a complex of problems. In fact, we are, if anything, moving further from a solution because the problem is becoming greater, not less. The number of students in our tertiary institutions is increasing, the amount of literature is increasing, the size and complexity of libraries is increasing, and, at the same time, librarians have come to realize that a satisfactory and successful programme of instruction in the use of libraries and literature is a much more subtle, complex and time consuming business than it was formerly thought to be. The hoped-for panaceas are either not materializing or proving illusory. Funds for hiring sufficient staff to maintain suitable programmes are less likely to be forthcoming now than they were five years ago and technology – the white hope – has been found by those who have used it to have serious limitations. It is time now for rigorous research instead of mere experimentation and for some fundamental reappraisal of basic assumptions.

Clark quoting Scrivener[8]

Considering the small numbers of professional librarians employed in most of these colleges (i.e. of higher and further education and colleges of technology) one must express surprise that any user education programmes are to be found in their libraries at all. . . . It would be unfair to suggest that their (i.e. tutor librarians) placement on these (i.e. Burnham) scales stimulates or underwrites the programmes of user education, or even that the programmes are inspired by the hope that they will be recognized as an entrée to such scales, but it is a fact that might be kept in mind. At any rate, it is a factor that somtimes pushes user education into the politics of college libraries and their parent institutions.

Malley[9]

These two substantial quotations span more than a decade but they summarize effectively the task still facing librarians in our kinds of institutions and set it in its political and professional context within the institution. A daunting exercise, but one which must be addressed constructively if the library's role is to be relevant to the college system and its clientele. How are we to create an appropriate strategy for the education and orientation of library users so that they come to regard the library as a friendly place and use it confidently and as a matter of course to supply their many information needs? 'A library must be socially and intellectually accessible' Ruddock.[10]

orientation is not just concerned with cognitive objectives but also with affective objectives aimed at creating an atmosphere for effective communication between user and libraries, at creating certain attitudes towards libraries on the part of the user and presenting an image of libraries as helpful friendly institutions.

Stevenson[11]

The library in a college is a major learning resource tool and as such must be made accessible to students to assist them in their learning, both the formal course programme leading to qualifications and the less formal 'learning for life' skills.

The complexity of the learning process

There is an increasing belief that the curriculum can be defined as a 'process' rather than purely in terms of a 'product'. This places emphasis on the ways people think and learn and moves away from notions of a body of knowledge or information to be acquired. The traditional view of learning resources meeting the needs of a pre-specified file of information is inadequate. Attention must be given to the ways students learn and the organization of such experiences.

McGettrick[12]

Learning is not a mechanical process and the tools that facilitate learning should not be applied mechanically.

Markless[13]

If librarians are to prove relevance to the curriculum they must look at how students learn and how the library can contribute to that process.

Biggs[14]

There have been many studies on the complexity of the learning process and the various levels at which students participating in the same learning exercise will accept and accommodate the body of knowledge that the teacher is attempting to convey. (Indeed the concept that learning is necessarily about the acquisition of a body of knowledge per se can no longer be accepted as the whole task vis-à-vis student learning.) 'Cognitive psychology holds that each individual's cognitive structure and processing skills are unique and there is considerable evidence to show that individuals have different "cognitive styles" or patterns of learning skills' Lawless.[15] Laurillard,[16] however, found that students changed their styles of 'learning . . . according to their perceptions of the demands of a particular learning task'. Ford:[17]

At a basic level, it is an axiom of modern learning theories that the meaningfulness of learning depends on the extent to which new information can be successfully linked to the learner's existing knowledge stored in memory. Such a principle underlines approaches to teaching from Skinner's[18] advocacy of small steps and careful sequencing in 'programmed learning' to Ausubel's[19] proposed 'advance organizers', in which linking bridges are laid between new information to be learned and the learner's existing knowledge, and to Pask's[20] stressing of the importance in learning of analogies, by which the unknown is learned via the known.

Ford[21,22,23,24] has written several detailed and well researched papers on various aspects of this subject. Of special significance for our present consideration are:

1 An article[25] that highlights the need for a cooperative approach across the college and a constant evaluation, pointing up the librarian's academic/non-academic role confusion that hampers progress in so many institutions:

> The gist of what I shall argue is this:
> (a) Teaching and learning must be the concern of a team of people including students, teachers, librarians, educational technologists and counsellors, all of whose roles are vital to learning.
> (b) On-going research and development by such a team is necessary for the evaluation and improvement of teaching and learning from the point of view of a cost effectiveness in both the short and the longer term.

The argument is exemplified by means of a case study based on a library-orientated student project with the concluding observation:

> How then, can one define the 'academicness' of the role of staff in an institution of higher education? A definition which centres round the qualifications of teaching staff would seem inviable. . . . It would be extremely difficult to assess the contribution to specific learning outcomes of individual, or groups of teaching or non-teaching staff . . . the roles of academic librarians, educational technologists and counsellors in learning can more than hold their own with that of class contact.

2 A series of articles[26,27] reviewing recent studies of learning in which research results have shown 'greater relevance to the study of library organization and use than were previously available, allowing a closer integration of the fields of librarianship and education'.

Ford's review begins to suggest the complexity of the learning process and indicates how some of the recent educational advances (e.g. resource-based learning, individualized learning, project work and independent study programmes) have added to this complexity and how equally the increasing diversification of the library operation increases the problem.

He sees this as a new challenge for librarians:

Reluctance to join what has been termed the educational technology or resource centre 'bandwagon', whilst open to interpretation at the time as a failure to realize that the *challenge to librarians* was pitched at a higher level than merely the provision of multi-media resources, namely at a level of a 'systems approach' to education, may now in retrospect, I would argue, be interpreted as the librarian's (intuitive) realization that considerations of teaching and learning operate at an even higher level of complexity than a 'systems approach' coupled with 'behavioural objectives'.

However, current research, which reflects more realistically the complexities of student learning, is beginning to pose another *challenge to librarians* (currently being taken up with the increasing interest in 'user studies' and the integration of librarianship and education courses), and to highlight the need for a further definition of 'librarianship' in the context of the provision of academic library services, the education of librarians and research into librarianship.

He argues the need for a research 'model' for 'library learning' in an attempt to extend present research and evaluation which tends to concentrate on the more easily quantifiable aspects of the operation:

Librarians have responded to the challenge of audio-visual media, and are responding well to the increasing need to justify levels of expenditure in quantitative terms. Perhaps an even greater challenge will be to fight against oversimplified quantification in justifying their activities, by being aware of the limitations of what may be highly *reliable* but not particularly *valid* methodologies for assessing their worth, and by developing research methodologies which do permit their worth to be more realistically measured. It is likely that intuitive support will decline with increasing competition for scarce funds. However, it is equally likely that much empirical research evidence existing at present does less than justice to the benefits of libraries. Some balance will be needed, and I would argue that a broad-based model of 'library learning' may be a prerequisite to the development of research methodologies uniting quantitative and qualitative measures of what libraries contribute in terms of student learning.

3 Ford's[28] later studies which are particularly concerned with the value of metacognition and critical thinking and express concern at the damaging effect of 'institutionalized education involving . . . a relatively meaningless, extrinsic "going through the motions" of learning in order to obtain a paper qualification as opposed to acquiring personally useful and valued information and skills.

The specific role and responsibility of the librarian is pointed up, particularly in relation to user education. The argument is forceful and cannot be summarized meaningfully in a brief quotation but the conclusion reached is significant:

Librarians must be more forceful in defining and pushing their own aims and objectives, framed in terms of the level, quality and scope of student learning. Many of these aims may be distinct from – perhaps even conflicting with – those drawn up by other parties in an educational institution. Librarians must be fully committed to developing institutional aims and objectives involving discussions of such complementary but often conflicting points of view. They have a unique and valuable viewpoint.

Educational objectives

Considerable attention has been given to the need for defining objectives over the past two decades or so and there is a considerable literature on the subject. Therefore it is perhaps surprising that there are still colleges that have not undertaken the exercise. Turner[29] in his article on staffing policy for college libraries, written as recently as 1984, suggests that vagueness is still evident on occasions:

> In practice it is likely that the library with no explicit and agreed objectives is likely to be staffed and resourced according to vague, often conflicting implicit objectives buried in the subconscious of college management.

Biggs[30] even more recently observes that . . . 'we find librarians using the term objectives very loosely and then usually to describe management rather than educational objectives'.

We have already stressed the need for the library to provide a system relevant to college and student needs. This will be more difficult if the college's own objectives are not clearly perceived and stated. Some of these will necessarily be management objectives:

> Establishing a set of objectives and agreeing them with college management will help to clarify attitudes within the institution. Furthermore, it is a step towards making college management more conscious of the library and more demanding of it – always the first step towards improving resources.
>
> Turner[31]

Resources in realistic proportion to the overall college budget and to the standards required of the library service are essential but resources of themselves do not guarantee a relevant service – they must be deployed and managed effectively.

In order to be able to do this the librarian and his team must have a clear understanding of the educational objectives of the parent institution and must be able to 'translate' these into meaningful library objectives. This is not an easy task. Biggs,[32] concerned primarily with evaluation of library services, points up some of the difficulties especially if we see the library as part of the 'learning' rather than the 'teaching' process. Quoting Derbyshire and Sheen[33] she considers that in order to assess effective use of any resources 'we can only do so sensibly by looking at the achievement of the objectives for which the resources are intended.' He (Derbyshire) suggests we begin by asking 'what are the company's objectives?' or as Sheen puts it 'what business are you in?' Further into his paper Sheen states:

asked of a traditional college the answer is simple – we are in the teaching business. Suppose, however you convince staff that we are *not* in the teaching business but in the *learning* business, or more accurately in the business of providing learning opportunities and support – then we are playing a different ball game. . . . If libraries are to be valued they must evaluate themselves and decide what business they are in even if there is no clear statement from the institution. In those enlightened institutions which have stated aims and objectives this job may be made easier or not depending upon how the library is seen to fit into the objectives.

We maintain that if the managers of college libraries wish to look forward and be relevant, then they *must* be in the business of learning in the context argued by Biggs and outlined earlier in this chapter and must ensure that the library service is seen to match closely the college's objectives.

The prevailing climate which has shifted the emphasis of control of the learning process from teacher-centred to student-directed, introducing a greater degree of flexibility and openness, makes this task less easy to define. Relevance becomes a more elusive quality requiring constant monitoring, feedback and modification.

Donovan's[34] approach, in which he sees the library as a vital resource and the librarians' expertise at exploitation and effective utilization of the sources as an intrinsic part of this, seems to be leading us in the right direction. The kind of questions he asks are 'How many students are *using* the library? How are they using it? What courses are library users following? What are the links between library and other staff?' These replace the more usual evaluation by gathering of issue, membership and stock statistics. For perhaps the first time there is an attempt to judge the service in terms of quality and relevance rather than in quantitative measures.

Chambers[35] writing on the college library and its contribution as 'an instrument for the achievement of educational objectives' quotes very specific examples whilst agreeing that library objectives must be determined within the individual college.

These educational considerations find expression in a number of ways but most will, in their detail, relate the levels of performance expected from the library to the requirement that students should be able to learn effectively in order to achieve stated course objectives.

In Chapter 4, which considers educational technology, we examine the purpose of educational objectives and attempt to define student satisfaction. It is important that librarians understand the nature and purpose of educational technology. If user education programmes are to be successful they must take account of it.

This aspect of the librarian's work is yet another in which closer cooperation with the teaching staff, involvement with curriculum development and course planning is required. Even in those colleges where positive relationships exist, response and reaction must be constantly modified to adjust to an ever-changing situation.

'Accessibility' of the service

The emphasis so far has been placed on the need to look out from the library's perceived boundaries and relate to its wider environment. Perhaps the time has arrived when we can allow ourselves a period of introspection. Having armed ourselves with a clear perspective of what business we are in and what we are attempting to achieve, we need to look at the existing system in a practical way and assess the 'status quo' – how relevant is the existing service? Where can improvements be made? How can we maximize on the use of existing resources? These are some of the questions we should set ourselves. Since our immediate concern is user education let us make the question very specific: 'How easy is it for the "average" student to use the library as it is at present?'

We may consider as over-simplistic the point of view iterated by Stevenson:[36]

> that the necessity for user education is of the librarian's own making; that there is a communications barrier between the librarian and the user that needs to be overcome. Much library induction is only rendered necessary by the complexity and inefficiency of the systems employed by librarians.

But there is a note of warning being sounded and it would be difficult to disagree with his statement that:

> The first task of any user education programme should be to ensure that the systems are effective, straightforward and self explanatory.

Attention should be paid to elementary matters like the existence and correctness of floor plans of the library, shelf and tier guiding. Are the printed guides up-to-date on such details as hours of opening, ticket allocations? Do they say where the libraries are situated? (Elementary matters but they can get overlooked when changes are made.) Do all pieces of equipment intended for users to operate themselves have simple, clear operational instructions? Does the catalogue have 'how to use' instructions, jargon-free and brief enough to be of practical value? Users will give up after the second sentence of a short essay or a complicated explanation!

It is quite a useful exercise to try and put oneself in the place of an average student visiting the library as a newcomer and to attempt an objective assessment. It can be revealing to talk to a new library assistant shortly after his arrival about these basic matters.

Stevenson[37] opines: 'I think the worst thing that happened to libraries was the Anglo-American Cataloguing Rules', and one can see his point. Whether one goes all the way with his opinion or not, the complexity of some library catalogues can be bewildering – even for some researching librarians visiting a different institution – to say nothing of how some of our college libraries' less academic clients must feel. Following a set of international rules, it is argued, makes for consistency within an organization and a degree of familiarity between different organizations but this is a very questionable argument. A commonsense approach and the needs of the library's own users must be the first consideration with attempts being made to balance the degree of detail against ease of use.

The library tour

The traditional library tour conveys so many facts that most are forgotten in a short time.

Moon[38]

Having 'put the house in order' as far as plans and guides are concerned the library tour will now be a more relevant exercise. However, it needs to be subjected to the same examination that has been suggested for library guiding. For example, the value must be questioned of the guided tour that takes groups of fifteen or more students round the library during the first week of term when they are already overwhelmed by a plethora of new circumstances and cannot readily relate the exercise to their ensuing course of study. How much, for example, do the YTS students at the back of the group understand (or care?) about a description of a library catalogue that they cannot see properly, and how much is this really an exercise in filling in another half hour of the induction programme to get them off some other lecturer's hands for a while? By the time the exercise has been repeated a few times in the day by the same guide it probably begins to lose its sense of reality and an infectious feeling of boredom may be the only lasting impression that students take away.

Our approach to this first exercise should be modified according to the type of student and the course being followed but location of the library site(s), together with the conveying of the library's general place in the college scheme and the creating of an impression that librarians and libraries are 'user-friendly', is probably as much as one ought to attempt at this stage with a promise of more specific help later when the time is right.

Sadly, both the library and the librarian have often in the past acquired a bad image in the minds of many staff and students. This may or may not have been deserved. What we must ensure is that in the present and future college library it most certainly is not. The best publicity is a good library service, a welcoming atmosphere where students and college staff feel stimulated and encouraged to research and work as opposed to one where they feel they are impeding the staff in the perpetuating of their 'mystic rites'!

With the advent of new technology, approaches other than a simple conducted tour have been tried. These range from tape/slide presentations at various levels of sophistication, 'Walkman' sets for individual use to computer-aided instruction and interactive video. These undoubtedly have some value when used in appropriate contexts but the disadvantages are that they are costly and time-consuming to produce, soon become dated, allow little or no active participation by users and miss the opportunity for personal contact between librarian and user.

There is scope for the use of information technology with some aspects of user education and we shall examine some of the possibilities later.

User education: active/passive, stand alone/integrated

The need for relevance is possibly nowhere more important than when considering user-education programmes. Students have far too many demands on their time and too many potential distractions for them to be prepared to spend any of it on library studies if they cannot see any point in the exercise. They may be short-sighted and need to be convinced, so programmes need to be structured in a way that will make an impact quickly and maintain it.

Race,[39] designing a course in study skills for students at the Polytechnic of Wales, acknowledges these points:

> Students are naturally unwilling to alter their long-standing strategies unless they can see rewards to be gained, such as:
> ● A more 'normal' lifestyle when preparing for exams.

94

- More effective use of study time, producing more free time to be spent with an easy conscience in social and extra-curricular activities.
- A greater belief in the probability of success.

Therefore the course design has to accommodate [the following] general requirements:
- Be short enough that lecturers may be prepared to spare the time.
- Be seen by students to offer tangible benefits.

What are the relative merits of the various approaches? Are there advantages in a series of library lessons built into a general studies or communications course? Are there benefits from giving all library studies a subject orientation? Is it feasible to involve students actively in 'doing' to aid and reinforce learning? With limited time available and the scarcity of library staff, is this too time-consuming? These are some of the questions librarians need to be asking themselves. The answers will be conditioned by local circumstances and have considerable implications as far as resourcing and cooperation with teaching departments are concerned.

There are strong arguments in favour of relating library studies to project work in the subject area especially with students on day release, sandwich or other work-related courses, but it should not be overlooked that increasingly education is concerned with social aspects and life skills, careers are no longer pursued for a life-time. This means that attention should be paid to skills transfer and continuing education over the whole life-span. The library has an important part to play in achieving these educational objectives.

> The complexity of information requirements in society amongst children and adults, in families, at work, in employment and at leisure, places on education a responsibility to provide tangible evidence of the diversity of information resources available and to provide structured learning opportunities for pupils and students to acquire skills in identifying, seeking, finding and using information.
>
> Sked[40]

> Study and information skills are inextricably linked with teaching methods and classroom management. Some help can be given in pastoral or general eduational time, but subjects are the 'crucial contributors'. It remains true that in most pupils' eyes . . . subjects are where the 'real' learning takes place.
>
> Tabberer[41]

Like Tabberer, Markless and Lincoln[42] come down firmly on the side of relating library studies to the curriculum for them to succeed. The work is directed at a secondary school audience but has much relevant advice for those working in the college library environment and its programmes are structured in a way that leaves scope for individual adaptation and interpretation.

There are several published models of course- or project-orientated library skills teaching programmes, e.g. *Examples of Library Work for TEC and BEC Courses* (LA CoFHE Group 1980) and many unpublished related to specific courses in individual colleges modified with course change and in the light of experience in use. The package that the present writers found to be the most effective and most relevant was that structured cooperatively for a specific group of students on a specific occasion as a collaborative effort between librarian and course tutor or, on some occasions, as a three-way process with general/communications studies tutor in cooperation with the subject tutors. The success of this approach can be ascribed to the fact that a specific need was clearly identified so that the course of study could be tailored in a manner that made it very relevant and the students therefore more likely to be motivated. However such programmes are highly expensive in terms of staff time and it is difficult to measure their cost-effectiveness. In addition, this approach depends on the teaching staff being convinced of the relevance and value of library user education for their students and on their cooperation in such matters as ascertaining in advance the availability, in the library's stock, of materials in sufficient quantity for the project and assignment exercises which they set their students.

Until libraries are more staff-intensive, the problems of evaluation better researched, and user education is generally recognized as an intrinsic part of the curriculum, we shall be faced with pragmatic compromises. Political considerations of counting teaching hours and problems of ordering priorities in overcrowded syllabuses have to be overcome before user education can be introduced into colleges in a systematic and planned way. However, it is important that we acknowledge the needs and consciously work towards their resolution.

Information technology and user education
Detailed consideration is given in Chapter 7 of the many functions and implications of information technology as it relates or may relate to the college library. Observations here will relate specifically to user education. Influences of IT on user education programmes undertaken in the college library will be broadly three-fold.

1   Hardware
Because of the growing volume and complexity of multi-media

resources in the library, it is necessary to give instruction and guidance in the use of the associated hardware. This means ensuring the existence of clearly worded instructions readily and obviously accessible with the assurance that staff are on hand when things go wrong – so that frustration and lack of confidence are not allowed to become a deterrent to use. It should also mean that verbal guidance and demonstrations are given as part of induction or more detailed course instruction. The pacing of this will be conditioned by student levels and the nature of the study courses, and will have to be judged according to immediate circumstances. Individual demonstrations are time-consuming so once more there are restraints in practice. However, user education in this area must be seen as an important aspect of the librarian's role if investment in the technologies is to be fully realized and the library is to achieve its potential as part of the college's open interactive learning resource.

2   *Automated bibliographical/information sources*

Many library information sources are already easily available in the form of data banks either with the library as a direct subscriber or through networks and gateways. With the increasing availability of compact disc and interactive video, this will become more and more the case, even in relatively small library systems. Increasingly library user education programmes will need to be concerned with making students aware of the range and existence of these sources and offering guidance in efficient data bank searching.

As the library's own management systems are transferred on to automated sources students will need to be made familiar with at least some of them if, for example, library catalogues and current awareness services are to be readily accessible to them.

3   *Computer-aided learning*

Software packages, both commercially produced and in-house varieties, have their place in many of today's college libraries and will certainly do so in the libraries of the future. If they are to be successful as an adjunct or sometimes a replacement for the book and journal as an extension of classroom learning reinforcement, and if we are seriously involved with the business of open and flexible learning, user-education programmes must feature them sufficiently for students to come to accept them as a resource which they find as accessible as the printed word and which they are prepared to use as a matter of routine.

User education programmes on micro

Computer-aided learning (CAL) can be used in a similar way to tape/slide presentations as the medium of delivery for the user-education programme itself. Some of the criticisms of audio-visual presentations made earlier apply equally to computer packages but there is more scope for interactivity though considerations of cost and time involved in making the packages could be a restraint.

Advantages may be seen in the fact that some of the more technically and less academically orientated students may be more motivated to use a computerized approach and be prepared to look at subject matter in which they would have shown no interest in a printed format. There is the additional merit of learning by doing, even learning from mistakes.

With the introduction of expert systems, use of the new technology should become less daunting for the diffident:

> phenomenal advances in new learning systems . . . were possible if educationists trainers and managers collaborated with the 'technologists' at the frontiers of advanced information technology. One of the features of the new systems was that they were not making people computer literate but making computers people-literate.
>
> Humphreys[43]

Herring[44] details some of the advantages and disadvantages concluding with the advice that:

> there is an important role (for new technology) but one which must not become more important than user education. We should look at our user education first and then look at technology to see if it can be applied. The technology must not become an end in itself.

Herring stresses the need to involve as many staff as possible so that the approach is positive and wholehearted: 'an educated workforce efficiently uses new technology and an ignorant one becomes its victim'.

Attitudes

Several references have already been made to the need to create a 'comfortable' learning/working atmosphere in the library. Whatever materials we amass, however detailed and structured our user-education programmes, however well-guided our libraries, if that intangible thing 'atmosphere' is not right students will not come willingly to it and will not operate effectively within it. Unfortunately comfortableness and user-friendliness are qualities not easily defined, subjective in measurement and not the same thing to all people at all times.

However, it is not difficult for practising librarians to understand the nuance of what is being suggested here and to identify some of the factors which add to or detract from this sought-after ambience.

Much of this relates to the approaches and attitudes of the librarian and the library staff. (Perhaps the college had better be nameless where the writers have heard it remarked by lecturing staff that recalcitrant students were threatened with a visit to the library as a form of discipline!)

A non-librarian's observation:

> librarians are guardians of the evidence of man's achievement, but I hope they can encourage our students as acolytes rather than high priests so as not to overawe them.
>
> Fletcher[45]

And a librarian's comment:

> The significant factor about these (i.e. user education) programmes is that the type, scope and success of the entire scheme often depends entirely on the personality of the librarian who does the teaching.
>
> Hammond[46]

Recent research carried out in Australia and reported in *Australian Academic and Research Libraries*[47] appears to prove earlier theories that there are psychological barriers between students and library staff.

What can be done to dispel the image that librarians have as unapproachable disciplinarians? A reasonable attitude, being human and resisting the temptation to overwhelm and overawe with an overkill of information, jargon, expertise, will help. Perhaps as a preliminary exercise one might look again at library notices and see how many of the 'Readers must not' variety could be removed. Flexible learning environments with client and library staff discovering together some of the potential of the new technology may be the means of laying the ghost of the overbearing librarian once and for all!

References

1   Herring, J., 'Information technology and user education', a COPOL exchange of experience seminar, 25 March 1986 at Polytechnic of Central London, *Audiovisual Librarian*, 12, (3), 1986, 158.
2   Durie, J., 'The reformed librarie keeper', 1650, quoted in Clark, D. *et al., The travelling workshops experiment in library user education,* BLR & D reports, British Library, 1981, 1.

3   Cowley, J. (ed.), *Libraries in higher education,* Bingley, 1975, 15.
4   Malley, I., 'User education', in McElroy, A.R., (ed.), *College librarianship: the objectives and practice,* Library Association, 1984, 271-83.
5   Malley, I. and Moys, S., *Survey of audiovisual programmes produced for user education in UK academic libraries,* Loughborough, Infuse Publications, 1982.
6   Clark, D. *et al., The travelling workshops experiment in library user education,* BLR & D reports, British Library, 1981, sections 1 and 2.
7   op. cit. 6, 1.
8   Scrivener, J.E., 'Instruction in library use: the persisting problem', *Australian Academic and Research Libraries,* 3, (2), 1972, 87-119.
9   op. cit. 4, 272.
10 Ruddock, J., 'Everybody is trying to do it without books', *CoFHE Bulletin,* 47, Summer, 1986, 2.
11 Stevenson, M.B., in Malley, I., (ed.), 'Educating the user', papers given at a two-day conference 16 and 17 November 1977, Library Association, 1979, 13.
12 McGettrick, B., 'What management expects of learning resources', *Learning Resources Journal,* LRDG, 2, (3), 1986, 96.
13 Markless, S. and Lincoln, P., (eds), *Tools for learning: information skills and learning to learn in secondary schools,* BLR & D report no 5892, British Library, 1986, 20.
14 Biggs, D., 'The college library: a valued resource?', *Education Libraries Bulletin,* 29, (1), 1986, 9.
15 Lawless, C. J., 'Evaluating the process of learning', in Percival, F., and Ellington, H., *Distance learning and evaluation: aspects of educational technology xv,* Kogan Page, 1981, 124.
16 Laurillard, D.M., 'The process of student learning', *Higher Education,* 9, 1979, 395-409. Copyright © 1979 by Martinus Nijhoff Publishers. Reprinted by permission of Kluwer Academic Publishers.
17 Ford, N., 'Reader services: for students, teachers and management', in McElroy, A.R. (ed.) op. cit. 4, 258.
18 Skinner, B., *Science and human behaviour,* Macmillan, 1953.
19 Ausubel, D. P., 'The use of advance organizers in learning and retention of meaningful material', *Journal of Education Psychology,* 51, 1960, 267-72.
20 Pask, G., 'Conversational techniques in the study and practice of education', *British Journal of Educational Psychology,* 46, 1976, 12-25.

100

21 Ford, N., 'Study strategies, orientations and "personal mean-ingfulness" in higher education', *British Journal of Educational Technology,* 10, (2), 1979, 143-60.

22 Ford, N., 'Levels of understanding and the personal acceptance of information in higher education', *Studies in Higher Education,* 5, (1), 1980, 63-70.

23 Ford, N., 'Recent approaches to the study and teaching of "effective learning" in higher education', *Review of Educational Research,* 51, (2), 1981, 345-77.

24 Ford, N., 'Quality in education for information: recent research into student learning', *Education for Information,* 1, 1983, 345-52.

25 Ford, N., 'Academic and non-academic roles in teaching and learning: a problem for librarians', *Journal of Further and Higher Education,* 5, (1), 1981, 24-9.

26 Ford, N., 'Cognitive psychology and "library learning"', *Journal of Librarianship,* 11, (1), 1979, 25-38.

27 Ford, N., 'Towards a model of "library learning" in education systems', *Journal of Librarianship,* 11, (4), 1979, 247-60.

28 Ford, N., 'Psychological determinants of information needs: a small-scale study of higher education students', *Journal of Librarianship,* 18, (1), 1986, 47-61.

29 Turner, C.M., 'Staffing: policy and problems', in McElroy op. cit. 4, 211.

30 op. cit. 14, 9.

31 op. cit. 29, 212.

32 op. cit. 14, 5.

33 Deboo, J. *et al.,* 'Value for money in further education', *Coombe Lodge Report,* 18, (1), 1985. Papers by Derbyshire and Sheen as quoted by Biggs, op. cit. 14, 5.

34 Donovan, K.G., *Learning resources in colleges: their organi-zation and management,* CET, 1981.

35 Chambers, F., 'Evaluating the college library: is it worth it?', *Coombe Lodge Report,* 19, (9), FESC, 1987, 587-600.

36 op. cit. 11, 10.

37 op. cit. 11, 20.

38 Moon, R., 'The library visit: evolution of a practical exercise', in City of London Polytechnic, *The part-time student in the library,* LLRS publications, 1983, 182.

39 Race, W. P., '"Help yourself to success" – improving polytechnic students' study skills', in Percival, F. and Ellington, H. op. cit. 15, 279.

40   Sked, M. J., 'Tertiary and secondary: relationships with school', in McElroy op. cit. 4, 79.

41   Tabberer, R., *Study of information skills in schools*, NFER-Nelson, 1986.

42   op. cit. 13.

43   Humphreys, C., 'Britain can lead the world with new stream of learner-friendly programs', report of seminar, Kingston upon Thames College of FE, October 1986, *Education*, 168, (15), 312.

44   op. cit. 1, 158.

45   Fletcher, E., 'New curricula: educational implications and impact on learning-centred resources', *Coombe Lodge Report*, 17, (3), FESC, 1984, 86.

46   Hammond, N., 'Teaching library use', in Cowley, op. cit. 3, 83.

47   'The psychological barriers between library user and library staff: an exploratory investigation', *Australian Academic and Research Libraries*, 17, (2), 1986, 63-9.

Chapter 7   Information technology and the library

Electronic communication is a rapidly changing subject. What is said may soon be out of date, and this is particularly true of examples of hardware and software packages. The purpose of this section is to try and show how IT will affect college libraries; technical details are kept to a minimum.

Developments in microtechnology affect us all. A few moments' reflection will show how much it has entered the daily lives of the authors. The draft of this book was produced using a wordprocessor package on a microcomputer. Since leaving full-time employment and working on our own, our largest capital investment has been in 'information technology'. In operational terms the two things most missed when leaving college were secretarial support and the photocopier. In order to operate as consultants and to provide executive and publishing services these had to be replaced. Investment was made in a desktop photocopier which uses sealed replacement cartridges thereby almost eliminating the need for servicing. The lack of secretarial support was overcome by buying a microcomputer, printer and appropriate software. The fact that both of us became engaged in many professional activities has led to us buying a second compatible micro. This equipment is used daily and is essential to our professional activities. It is as much a part of our daily lives as the TV, stereo equipment, the freezer or the microwave. Perhaps one should also note in passing that many consumer durables including some of those just quoted will have microelectronic devices incorporated in them.

Continuing this 'biographical' note we should point out that although we are still practising professional librarians, we are also library users. For the first time in many years we no longer have libraries which are 'ours' to use at will. So we have access to an academic library to which we travel some distance and to whose regulations for external readers we must conform. We use that library for specific academic and professional purposes and, in so doing, are exposed to their systems and the applied information technology they use. We also bring to the library certain understandings and expectations about information technology which we have developed consciously or have absorbed subconsciously.

In this we are not unique. Many library users have computer literacy, some to quite an advanced level. Among our younger students this will be in some degree due to their primary and secondary education and we would not want to underestimate the part schools have played. However, much of this understanding has been consumer- and marketplace-led rather than inspired by formal education.

Returning to our personal situation, much of what we do requires the use of wordprocessing but we also use an elementary form of database and have experimented with a spreadsheet. If we choose, we can have on-line banking and building society facilities in the home. As with most other customers we make more visits to the computerized cash dispenser outside the bank door than transactions involving face-to-face contact with the staff inside. The theatres we visit more often than not take our booking by computer and issue a printout ticket. Our dentist operates his appointment system on an in-house database, the doctor's group practice does not, but it's only a matter of time.

The point behind these remarks (the examples quoted could be extended almost limitlessly) is that our college libraries are already providing services to intelligent and inquiring young (and not so young!) people whose enthusiasm for the new technology is almost certainly going to have been fired by the developments in information technology going on around them. The pace of this development and our clients' exposure to it will increase steadily with the passage of time. As with the audio-visual and video explosion which preceded it we may well see the phenomenon of our professional educators being less self-confident and less willing to learn about and apply information technology than the students they teach. In the past, teachers were 'information-rich' in a world that was 'information-poor'. That situation has been reversed. The amount of information has increased dramatically and, even more importantly, it is much more accessible. Thus the learner given the right techniques and access can be as rich in information as his teacher. This has fundamental implications for the role of the teacher and his relationship with students. In the future the selection and rejection of information will be as important as the acquisition of knowledge. Learning will be able to concentrate on the interpretation and use of knowledge provided that the learner is proficient in the skills of handling and retrieving information.

The college librarian and information technology
The impact of information technology on libraries is a combination
of the application of developments in computer, telecommunication
and video technologies This means that libraries are at the beginning
of a period of rapid change. In recent years a considerable body of
professional literature has grown up about the impact of information
technology on libraries and its likely effect upon librarians. This book
deals specifically with college libraries; readers who wish to look at
the subject more generally should consult one of the more general
surveys. Among the most recent is William Masterson's *Information
technology and the role of the librarian.* It deals with the nature of
librarianship in the 'information age' but it reflects the author's
academic library background. We suggest at the present time
information technology is most likely to affect the college librarian in
four ways:

1   The provision of software and hardware for students to use.
This will be for four main purposes:
- To gain familiarity in the use of computers – initially import-
  ant, but probably a decreasing use.
- To support teaching by accessing prescribed software.
- For individual learning and inquiry – computer-assisted and
  computer-based learning.
- For students to produce their assignments for assessment (as
  an alternative for those who do not have their own personal
  computer).

2   As a means of accessing information held in databases and
transmitting that information to clients. At present this is almost
exclusively bibliographical but in the not-too-distant future we may
have textual transmission as a practical proposition and sufficiently
low-cost to be relevant to further education.

3   The automation of library housekeeping routines, principally
the order and receipt of materials; cataloguing and the production of
bibliographic tools; issue and retrieval. These, either introduced
separately or through an integrated package, are likely to be the most
immediate concern of many college librarians.

4   In-house production of documents. The current interest in
desk-top publishing could offer librarians possibilities for much
better and immediate in-house information both bibliographical and
for user familiarization.

The provision of hardware and software for students to use
This is the aspect that has most in common with the provision of

other multi-media facilities in the modern library/resource centre. There are important distinctive features because of the interactive nature of the technology. Provision of this kind will depend on the college policy towards the provision of computing facilities and the relationship between the library, the computer service and academic departments. If there is a coordinated learning resources service then, in theory, it should be easier to work out the respective provision between the library and the computer centre. A clear college policy towards the provision of learning facilities is essential, together with a proper definition of the funtion of the library and the computer unit. The degree of centralisation/decentralization of resources has also to be decided, balancing the immediacy of access with the highest effective level of use of expensive hardware and software. In computer provision, forms of networking may go a long way towards reconciling this apparently insoluble conflict.

Broadly speaking the computer service in its provision of hardware and software will provide a central service of equipment purchase, maintenance and loan to departments to cover their teaching needs and specialist subject use. This will be in addition to its own centre-based computers for courses in computing. The provision of software by the computer service will probably also reflect this although departments will often have greater autonomy in building up their own collections of specialist programmes. The provision in the library will have to try and meet the following needs:

- Individual reference/reinforcement of subject teaching, i.e. copies of departmental programmes for students to follow up in their own time.
- Individual practice in the skills of computer software handling, e.g. wordprocessing, spreadsheet and database use.
- Support for computer-based learning and independent study.
- The opportunity for students to produce their own written and other practical assignments using the computer as a tool.

The software will need to be accompanied by the appropriate hardware. This faces the library with a decision. How far does it go in providing an environment for computer use within the library? Factors that will influence this decision are:

- Is this being provided elsewhere in college, e.g. in the computer centre?
- Is there sufficient demand for this kind of provision from within college? This is an important factor when choices have to be made by management about the deployment of finance.

- Is there space in the library for such a development without adversely affecting the other services?
- Has the librarian sufficient imagination, drive and managerial ability to achieve it? Is he able to relate to the head of computing to plan this as part of the overall college strategy for computer provision?

The increasing impact of information technology on learning and the greater amount of educational software will lead to an expressed need in colleges. If the library is going to play any significant part in meeting this demand it must consider provision as a whole. Merely to store software on its shelves would be to stand aside from the main thrust of this *interactive* medium.

Access to database information and textual transmission
This is likely to be an aspect which will become of increasing interest and use to college libraries. Education librarians are already used to bibliographic databases such as Blaise-Line and ERIC although cost will probably limit the amount of use most colleges will make of these national and international tools in the immediate future. It is worth noting that as well as general bibliographical databases some are now appearing which are of particular relevance to British education. For example, it is planned to have an on-line version of the British Education Index available in Summer 1988.

In addition a whole range of other information is rapidly becoming available as the recent *Education* digest 'Databases for education'[2] makes clear. It quotes from the recent report of the Information Technology Advisory Panel (ITAP):[3]

> We see IT as a way of tackling the problems which our existing educational system faces through the explosive growth in knowledge which is under way. Within IT itself it has been estimated that the available knowledge has been increasing at such a rate that less than half of the information currently available existed three years ago.

The most well known and generally used host databases are the Teletext services, CEEFAX and ORACLE together with the GPO's Prestel. In education PRESTEL started their Prestel Education Service in 1985 which is intended to collate all existing training and education information. Additionally there is the Times Network Service (TTNS) and a relatively new database service, National Educational Resources Information Service (NERIS), which aims to draw together information about learning materials and their availability.

A number of national and regional databases have recently been developed. Among the national databases is the Educational Management Information Exchange (EMIE), a database containing information on matters of educational policy and practice set up by the Information, Research and Development Department of NFER. Another national database is FERN (Further Education Research Network) which is an electronic research network for FE teachers and has been designed to include teleconferencing facilities. A service with which many college librarians will already be familiar is MARIS (Materials and Resources Information Service) providing information about open learning packages in craft, technician, supervisory and management education. An interesting example of a local database is the Isle of Wight College Viewdata System. This includes details of college courses, departments, library information, the Isle of Wight Domesday project, together with local information (such as entertainment, island places of interest, job vacancies and general community information). Proposed future developments include adding local county council information; expanding the Viewdata Keyword Search facility on the system; examining open learning via on-line systems; setting up a schools library of available software on a local basis.

Databases also exist in particular areas of education. An important database with a curriculum focus is the Education Counselling and Credit Transfer Information Service (ECCTIS). This provides details of educational courses in advanced, further and higher education in the UK. A detailed account of this service by John Taylor[4] appears in the *Learning Resources Journal* including the implications for learning resources. Reference is made later to the compact disc version currently being introduced.

An interesting venture in multicultural education has been started at Bulmershe College of Higher Education. This is AIMER (Access to Information on Multicultural Educational Resources) which contains details of multicultural ephemera and non-commercially available materials.

In the 14 to 19 area of educational provision MSC, TVEI and FEU have all set up databases. The FEU has set up two databases, 'Resources for Information' and 'Technology in Further Education', as part of a project for the development of a courseware system for further and higher education. Another valuable tool for research and development workers in the field of disability is the British Database on Research into Aids for the Disabled (BARD).

Reviewing this explosion of activity the *Education* digest[5] says:

Education's response to this situation has been to seek ways of developing the full range of handling skills of their pupils – using existing resources to develop retrieval skills and creating databases to develop information-handling and processing skills.

Advisers and administrators, in addition to teachers and lecturers, have recognized the value of information systems to support them in their work. The addition of a modem and communication software to the one humble micro has enabled them to access remote databases and to conceive plans for local and regional networks.

Accessing the database

It is possible already to use microcomputers as tools to access this immense amount of information available on a number of major online services. The cost of the additional software and hardware is likely to be acceptable to colleges provided they see sufficient advantage in having the facility.

Once the library can access the host database it can then download information onto a floppy or hard disc. This enables the library to use the material for its own purpose. It can:

- Modify the material for its own in-house use (by reformatting or wordprocessing). This would be useful if you wanted to use the information in a particular format in college.
- Use the records from more than one database to build up a more extensive report.
- Build up an in-house database. (*Note:* this would require the agreement of the database producer.)

As well as downloading one can reverse the process and upload. This means sending messages and reports out. This could be used for transfer of messages and orders or for fast delivery via electronic mail. Although such uses in college libraries may seem to be an exercise in futurology such is the pace of change that they may be nearer than one thinks. The forward-looking librarian would do well to become informed in these matters and to introduce perceptions of the developmental implications into his future planning. Put more simply: find out; update your knowledge; introduce it into your developmental thinking. Do this for yourself *and* introduce it into the staff development programme for your other professional staff.

Anne Ramsden's articles in *Micromation News*[6] and the *Learning Resources Journal*[7] give considerable detail about the packages currently available and they are being added to all the time.

109

Software requirements
Ramsden says that the software must be able to:

1 Make the micro behave like a terminal (terminal emulator) i.e to transmit and receive data under certain specifications.

2 Deal with the idiosyncrasies of different telecommunication networks and different hosts when transferring data, whether uploading or downloading.

3 Store the log-on procedures required for the remote computer, e.g. network addresses, user identifiers, passwords etc., within the program.

4 Pre-store on the disc the search strategy and . . . allowing the user to adjust his search online if necessary.

5 Display data about to be captured on the screen, at the same time it can be recorded on disk for later display or printing after it is disconnected from the online service.

Hardware requirements
Assuming that you have a micro with disc storage the other items of hardware the online searcher requires are:

- Telephone
- Modem
- Communications interface

Your telephone will need to have the current type of sockets, which may necessitate modification to your existing system by British Telecom.

The modem is the means whereby data sent from the computer is translated into signals that can be sent over a telephone line to another computer. Some micros have an internal modem and you simply have to plug in to your telephone socket, otherwise you have to rent or buy a separate piece of equipment.

The communications interface acts as a gateway for signals transmitted back and forth from the microcomputer to the modem. It is a serial interface which means that when it is interfaced with a microcomputer (assuming it does not have a built-in modem) there must be an 'RS232C' port. There are many different models of communication interfaces and modem boards and care must be taken to ensure compatibility with your micro.

Software packages
There are a number of different types of communications software. Ramsden[8] identifies four main types with examples that are currently available:

1 General purpose communications software, usually designed for one range of machines, eg: Microstuf's CROSSTALK (MSDOS and PCDOS machines); ACT's COMMUNIQUE (Apricot); Perfect Software's PERFECT LINK (IBM and compatibles); Sagesoft's CHITCHAT is available on the Apricot, IBM PC and Datel (Torch).

2 Packages aimed at end users of particular online services, eg: SDC's ORBIT MASTER, Dialog's DIALOGLINK.

3 Packages with gateways to a wide range of hosts, eg: Head Computers' HEADLINE; Userlink's ASSIST; Learned Information's CONNECT; ESA-IRS's MIKROTEL

4 Front end packages designed to mask the end-user (businessmen, scientists, engineers etc.) from the logging-in procedures and the search commands required by the online host. This type of software usually restricts access to certain hosts. For example Userlink's IT gives access to Data-Star, Pergamon Infoline, ESA-IRS and Dialog: ISI's Sci-Mate gives access to Dialog, SDC, ISI and BRS.

Implications for the librarian

These packages are within the expenditure range of many colleges. While subscriptions to on-line services may still seem expensive they are coming down and as the cost of print-based material rises the financial limitations will become less of a barrier. Certainly college librarians should be giving serious consideration to the implications of using on-line services. Compared to print based tools they offer:

● More up to date material.
● Information that sometimes cannot be found elsewhere.
● In many cases a 'mediated' service through specialist information officers.
● Considerable savings in space compared with hard copy.
● In some cases offline prints.

Against this you have to consider:

● Accessibility – terminals can be less accessible than hard copy unless there is multiple provision.
● Possibility of technical malfunction.
● Expense.

Text transmission

So far we have been looking at the downloading of bibliographic information but the development of electronic mail and electronic publishing should not be overlooked. Textual transmission is being developed in commerce and industry and although it may seem a long way from the college world with its declining investment the pace of change is such that librarians should be making themselves aware of developments in this field. Electronic communication publications exist largely alongside print on paper in the so-called 'dual mode', however in addition to this there are an increasing number of publications that exist only in machine-readable form. They have not and never will be issued in print. Lancaster[9] suggests that it's only a question of time before we move to the complete evolution of electronic publishing and in the study undertaken by Lancaster, Drasgow and Marks[10] there are some specific forecasts *on a worldwide basis* including:

- By the year 2000, 50% of existing abstracting/indexing services will be available only in electronic form . . .
- Existing periodicals (in science and technology, social sciences and the humanities) will not reach . . . the 25% level of conversion [to electronic forms] until after 2000.
- By 1995, 50% of newly issued technical reports will only be available in electronic form.

Consider the implications for the practising librarian. The year 2000 is only a few years away. Given a working expectancy up to the age of sixty-five any librarian under the age of fifty-three can expect to see these forecasts fulfilled in his working lifetime (always assuming they are correct!). Put another way, a young librarian just starting his career can expect to see these developments take place by his early thirties and look forward to up to another thirty years of professional activity.

Interactive video and compact discs

Compact discs

One of the features of the latest developments in information technology is the coming together of audio, video and computer technology. Fay[11] suggests the trend towards an integrated system is well on the way:

The trend is obvious, the storage available on the desk top continues to grow and the cost to fall, the graphics capability of systems will grow with the increase of memory and the power of the processor. Put five MIPS, a couple of megabytes and a megapixel display together and a new breed of device is in sight. Data storage using the technology in your compact disc player is available now. It cannot be long before the advantage of putting all these elements together results in a real multimedia educational delivery system, with stereo sound, moving pictures of TV quality, facsimile texts and computer-generated text, all presented according to a scheme you have defined and in response to the learning pattern of the individual student. The system will be available on your personal computer, maybe your PC, and sooner than you think.

Fay refers to data storage on compact disc and this is the latest technological development used by ECCTIS (Educational Counselling and Credit Transfer Service), the information service for those looking for course information in further and higher education. The exploratory work has been done at the Open University to use the CD/ROM to produce a disc containing the complete ECCTIS database. The result, described by Taylor[12], is a medium that is easy and quicker to search without the costs (and hazards!) of on-line link-ups. Since Spring 1987 ECCTIS offers its guest database on an annual subscription with updated discs being provided at regular intervals.

While such a system does not give the same up-to-date service as an on-line system there are considerable advantages of immediacy and simplicity of access. With reduction in price of CD players as the volume on the market increases this becomes a practical proposition even for colleges with limited budgets. If the direction illustrated by ECCTIS is taken up by other databases offering bibliographic information then the librarian will have another route to access. The college librarian coming to grips with the implications of on-line searching may find that technology is offering him a more immediate and 'friendly' alternative.

Interactive video
Interactive video has been widely publicized, especially through the BBC Domesday Project. It is clear that linking a computer to a video disc gives a powerful and flexible information system that is truly interactive. The storage capacity of video discs (up to 324 Mbytes of digital data and 54,000 analogue video frames on the Domesday discs) is enormous and there is great potential for the reference book or collection. Examples include the Grolier Videodisc Encyclopaedia of Science & Technology and the UK National Medical Slide Bank. The reference resource is of immediate interest to the librarian but there are other uses which may in the future have a greater influence on the way in which the library is used.

Roach[13] suggests that among other types of interaction are forms of individual tutorial including problem solving; simulation; and commercial applications such as the 'point of sale' system. This is in effect a video disc catalogue of goods or services linked in with a computer program. Examples of this kind of use are given by Oldham:[14].

> Let us suppose . . . that we are a busy motor repair workshop. Our mechanics deal with hundreds of different models of cars and more particularly with many types of carburettors. We can put photographs, exploded diagrams and textual explanations for virtually every known type onto a single video disc and the mechanic can call up the desired segment almost instantly.
>
> Let us imagine we are travel agents. A customer wishes to select a summer holiday. We have a video disc and the relevant software is programmed into the computer built into the player. It is now simply a question of finding the appropriate track through the branching program. A beach holiday? England or overseas? Black Sea or Mediterranean? Spain or Italy? Costa del Sol or Costa Blanca? Torremolinos or Marbella? This hotel or that? And the 54,000 pictures, with text overlay, form an unrivalled data-bank.

Those who have direct experience of the Domesday system or have watched BBC television programmes about it will realize the range and variety of material to which one has access. Schools and colleges, says the BBC Information Pack, 'will have a discovery learning system on a scale never imagined before', libraries 'will have a rapid, interactive method of locating and comparing information from many disciplines'.

The implications for the librarian are two-fold. First it is an interactive reference tool with the ability to bring together print, visual images, still and in motion, together with sound. Alternatively it is a learning system which will have an impact upon the way in which your clients use the library. Its potential may be incorporated by the course planner into students' programmes. Such use could range from using it as another support to existing taught courses to devising new programmes of study with an increased element of individualized learning, the student interacting with the material on the video disc. The implications of this for the library may be less immediate but in the longer term they could be more far-reaching.

So far this sounds fine but interactive video is a complex medium and still relatively expensive. This is true of the hardware but as a 'one-off' the cost may be defrayed as a capital expenditure item. The problem is with the software. Apart from the encyclopaedic reference tool, will it be commercially viable to produce enough to give us an effective collection of resource material? How will these discs be updated? The possibility of producing new discs like new editions of books does not seem feasible on cost grounds and, as yet, discs cannot be modified. The alternative is to use tape but this is a slower, less permanent method. Oldham[15] suggests that the relative advantages and disadvantages between rival systems of tape and disc are:

Tape	Disc
Mastering less expensive	Mastering very expensive
Updating easy	Updating very difficult
In-house production possible	Needs professional production
Still picture – low quality	Still picture – high quality
Suitable for small-scale production	Only feasible with large-scale production

It is likely that the disc will be more user-friendly and have greater appeal for the student and resource-centre user. In saying this we must not overlook the potential of tape-based systems for low-cost and in-house production. An example of this of particular interest is the training package *Getting started: an introduction to microcomputers for librarians,* by Nancy Hammond.[16] The development of this package was funded jointly by the British Library Research and Development Department, Brighton Polytechnic Department of Librarianship and the Polytechnic of Central London Library Services. The package is intended to be used in one-day training sessions for library staffs usually with an input from the author. It expects that staff, after working through the programme, will be able to:

1 Identify and understand basic computer jargon.
2 List uses for computers in libraries.
3 List criteria to assess the needs of a particular library which can be met by the use of micros.
4 List types of software which have library applications.
5 List selection criteria for hardware and software.
6 Gain hands-on experience of the use of microcomputers and interactive systems.

These objectives illustrate the value of interactive video to further education in training based on a simulator, an aspect which is discussed by Steele:[17]

the training based on the [video disc] simulator is able to give the trainee experience of situations that might occur only once or twice a year in real life sitting next to an experienced operator. This type of video disc training is very cost-effective even though only a small number of trainees have to be trained each year. The actual quality of the training is improved, and the length of time before a trainee becomes competent is reduced. The simulator operates in a number of modes, including initial teaching, practice and testing for competence.

In the longer term, the other great value of interactive video is its potential to enhance independent learning. This development will depend on the availability of sufficient relevant and high-quality yet affordable software together with the commitment of colleges to independent learning and their ability to create courses which take advantage of the opportunities this medium offers.

Automating college library housekeeping systems
For many college librarians this is one of the most important professional questions exercising them at the present time. Hitherto we have been considering the impact of IT on the use of the library by staff and students but the organization and operation of library procedures is a particular area for the librarian and his staff. This is where the college expects the librarian to take the lead in initiating proposals and implementing them. The suitability of computer applications for library operations is both an advantage and a disadvantage. An advantage because in arguing the case for introducing library automation the librarian can build on a degree of general appreciation of the relevance of computers to library techniques. It could be a disadvantage if the preoccupation with housekeeping operations reinforces the image of the librarian as a backroom provider at a technical level.

With all that is written in the professional press and the range of courses and other staff development activities in this area one might assume that most colleges were some way along the automation path and many had already one or more of their basic systems operating by computer. As is often the case, the level of achievement is some way behind the discussion of innovation but change is taking place and its pace is increasing. Thirty five returns from a survey of colleges carried out by the Learning Resources Development Group in June 1986[18] revealed that 20 of these had some form of automated library operation. Almost all the remaining colleges expressed an interest in or an intention to introduce some form of micro-based library automation. Over half of these mentioned specific operations which they hoped to automate by March 1988. Paul Burton's annotated bibliography *Microcomputers in library and information services*[19] is an extremely useful source of information. In addition to the obvious sources of journals and monographs he points out that 'many librarians have described their efforts at "micro-automation", and they constitute a large proportion of the references listed'.

The housekeeping activities we are primarily concerned with are: acquisitions; cataloguing; issue systems. It is worth noting that in the survey mentioned above other activities listed included periodical organization and producing in-house bibliographies and indexes as well as on-line searching from databases.

Why automate?
We suggest three possible reasons:

1   To be in the vanguard of development and to be seen to be 'with it'.

2   Because your operation is expanding and automation is part of a planned development to facilitate this and to maximize the efficient use of staff releasing them from many repetitive routine tasks.

3   You cannot cope any longer using traditional manual methods. There is a crisis in at least one area of your operations and some form of automation seems to offer the only possible solution.

It would be easy to dismiss the first reason except that we are all tinged to some degree with professional egotism, even if we don't care to admit it! However in today's stringent financial climate the opportunity for professional self-indulgence is likely to be rare. No doubt we would like to believe that it is in response to the second reason that we are proceeding. Perhaps in some colleges this is true to some degree, would that life could be so logical and so planned! We expect, indeed we fear, that it is for the last reason – pushed by pressure and the need to do something about it – that most of us take the first hesitant steps along the road to automation.

Automating library services at Edge Hill College: a cautionary tale
Peter Pack

I recall the situation when, as Head of Learning Resources at Edge Hill College, I was approached by the senior library staff and told that the library issue system (dual slip which had served the college well for over ten years) could no longer cope with the strain of just on 100,000 issues per academic year from a bookstock of nearly 200,000 volumes. The choice was either to abandon the control and level of service of the existing system and replace it with something less complex and labour-intensive or to find an alternative way of providing the same level of operation. Automation seemed to be the way forward but in 1981 most systems were expensive mainframe- or minicomputer-based for large polytechnic and university libraries. The alternatives were either in-house systems developed on 8-bit home computers like the BBC micro or a small number of commercial library systems with very small capacity. Edge Hill was too big and the issue system too complex for either the in-house or small package development. On the other hand it could not afford the dedicated mini-based systems, nor had it the resources to undertake the simultaneous automation of all its housekeeping routines. At that stage there seemed to be nothing that really fitted our needs.

The break came almost by chance during a specialist adviser panel meeting at CNAA. A colleague who knew that we were investigating larger micro-based systems whispered to me that 'something interesting had been developed at Aston University and was now in use'. The result of this was that after discussions with Aston University and Macbeth Computers of Leamington Spa, who had originally installed the Aston system, Edge Hill College decided to purchase an automated issue system developed from the original Aston package and run on South West Technical Products' microcomputers using hard discs. The second break came early in 1983 when money became available at very short notice outside the normal revenue and capital estimates to puchase the hardware and software. Because our investigations and forward planning were sufficiently advanced we were able to take advantage of this windfall.

From then on our troubles began. We had been forced to move quickly to acquire the equipment and software; we now had to install and implement the system as soon as possible both to relieve the pressures on the library staff and show some customer benefit to the college to justify the investment that had been made. It was only then that the full enormity of the task of bar-coding those 200,000 books, while still maintaining the existing service and without any guarantee of additional input of labour, really hit us!

It would be tedious to detail events from then on. Sufficient to say that some additional temporary staff were found. A means of prioritizing categories of books to be processed was worked out. Staff training exercises were undertaken. The many other necessary tasks were carried out including the very important measures needed to prepare and familiarize the readers with the new procedures. When I left the college in September 1984 this task was still not complete, although the automated issue system became operational during the 1984-5 academic year.

There is a postscript to this story. It is reported in *Learning Resources News*, February 1987, that Edge Hill College is to upgrade its issue system from the Aston University system, which was the precursor to Information Systems Design's CIRC, to a full CIRC issue system based on Nimbus microcomputers. After two years of operation there has been sufficient development in the technology available to make it worthwhile to undertake a major upgrading which changes it to a system using a specialist commercial library package operating on standard hardware.

This may seem a drastic move after such a short time but it underlines the pace of change and the need for institutions to accept this in their thinking. Apart from having an automated issue system up and running for two years, what the college will have gained most will have been:

- A bar-coded and processed stock.
- A staff experienced in running such a system.
- Users who are familiar with and expect this type of service.

and because of this

- A readiness on the part of the college to upgrade the system and to make further investments in information technology in the library.

Learning the lessons

Do your homework: before a problem had been identified at Edge Hill, professional library staff were encouraged as part of their staff development to become fully acquainted with the application of computers to academic libraries. One positive outcome of this was Ruth Wilson's bibliography on library automation. Ruth was one of our assistant librarians; her task was to update herself and her colleagues by surveying the literature in the field. This was published initially in the college in 1983 and an updated version subsequently appeared in the *LRDG Bulletin*[20].

Once the need to automate had been decided on, one of our tutor-librarians was given the task of amassing further information specifically about computerized issue systems and this involved visits and discussions as well as reading. 'Homework' is required in two areas: the background of computers and libraries that we have already mentioned and the evaluation and assessment of your own library and the impact of new technology on it.

Evaluate the system

When you start on the process of automation the most important thing for the professional librarian is *not* knowledge of automated systems. This may sound like a contradiction but it is not meant to be. Certainly it helps enormously to have as much background as can reasonably be acquired but this is information about a tool, for that is what your automation package is. A tool is only useful when you know where and how you are going to use it – collecting tools of any kind for their own sake is an expensive and unprofitable pastime. Buying the wrong tools or those which are beyond your ability to use correctly is equally unsatisfactory. The college libraries of the UK, like any other professional activity, have cupboards where their skeletons are stored. They are reminders of ill-judged enthusiasms; of professional egotism at variance with considered need; perhaps of just plain gullibility in the face of the hard sell.

The answer lies in evaluating your system to identify its needs and to be able to ask the right questions about the suitability of any package to meet those needs. A good library will have an on-going policy of evaluation to ensure that it provides the best for its clients within the constraints of its resources. At Edge Hill College the librarians maintained a staff manual. I always admired the way in which this was updated and referred to, not as a straitjacket of rigid and pettifogging routines, but as a point of reference for consistency. It was also used creatively as a measure of existing practice that served as a point of departure when changes in demand suggested that adjustments were needed in terms of an operational response. This was never more clearly demonstrated than during the planning of the automated issue system. It was necessary to decide:

- Did we wish to change the operation or to automate our existing procedures?
- What would the effect of automating one aspect of the housekeeping operations have upon the rest of the routines?
- What requirements were we going to put to the producers of the software package that were (1) desirable, (2) essential?
- Given the likely changes to the routine work to be undertaken how would this affect (1) staff deployment, (2) accommodation and furniture?

These longer-term considerations had to be kept clearly in mind and not obscured by the immediate pressures of trying to implement a major change with few additional resources at the same time as keeping the existing library service fully operational.

Prepare your specification
This follows logically from your evaluation and the quality of your preparation. The specification should be as thorough and well prepared as the librarian's brief to the architect for a new library building. A good specification will:

1   Demonstrate your professional approach to the software producer.

2   Enable the software producer to respond positively to your library's needs.

3   Help you to assess the quality and suitability of the package you are being offered. It should assist you through your discussions with the firm to get a fair idea of their ability to operate computer programs *in library terms.*

4   Enable you, from the manufacturer's responses, to form a fair opinion of his ability to support and update the system being offered.

5   Reduce the risk of omitting important information or needs which involve costly and time-consuming modifications later.

6   Respond positively and confidently to any advice that the manufacturer offers. Many of the library software producers have specialized in library systems design, some are professional librarians. Their advice can be invaluable since they can often bring comparative experience from other installations. If you know what you want you should be better able to assess the quality of what you are being offered.

Shop around

The last two years has seen a rapid growth in the range of systems suitable for college libraries. Pat Manson's survey in 1986[21] lists 16 suppliers of microcomputer-based library housekeeping systems and the situation is constantly changing. This means that systems are available for a range of colleges, not just the largest or those offering mainly advanced level courses. It also means that there are alternatives for the librarian to choose from. When we were investigating the situation at Edge Hill we were virtually in the position of working with a computer software firm and systems designer to produce an acceptable system. There is no doubt that the present librarian will have looked carefully and critically at all the alternatives before choosing the successor to the existing system.

In-house v specialist 'commercial' software

One source of advice is the college head of computer services. You may also decide to collaborate with him to develop in-house systems for library automation. It may be that this is necessary because of college policy that he should be responsible for all such developments. The LRDG survey[22] referred to earlier showed some twenty applications using either standard (as opposed to specialist library) software or in-house programes. At Edge Hill the views of the tutor i/c computing were sought from the beginning but there was never any real doubt on his part or the librarians' that we were going to need specialist software. His advice was helpful and supportive but the nature and complexity of the requirement was not within his college remit.

The advice of college computer specialists can be helpful in three contexts:

1 Determining the suitability and reliability of the hardware and software being offered in computing (as opposed to library operation) terms.

2 Offering advice about the educational aspects of the exercise. You may feel that this comes from other channels within the college (in any case this is 'housekeeping' rather than education). Nevertheless, the majority of college computer specialists are drawn from the ranks of teachers rather than systems analysts and their function usually includes a large coursework component. In this respect they have a relationship to college activities which is not dissimilar to some academic or tutor-librarians and could offer a particular view which might be stimulating and perceptive.

3 Relating the library system to the automation of other college information systems. To take a practical example, an issue system requires detail about readers. In a manual system these are normally entered by the reader on a registration card. In an automated system it is possible to incorporate such information from another data file provided that it already exists. The assistance of the head of computer services could be helpful in achieving this. This is a rather limited example but as college information systems are increasingly automated with networking offering multi access to data then the role of the library both as a contributor to and a user of that system must be borne in mind.

Having looked at ways in which collaboration can usefully take place, I am bound to say that I can envisage few situations where it would be sensible to develop an in-house scheme in preference to a commercial package. It would be a case of trying to reinvent the wheel and the likely outcome would be a less than satisfactory system which was prohibitively expensive in terms of the man-hours invested. Perhaps there are some attractions in terms of cost (and because they are already used elsewhere in college) of using a standard commercial database for cataloguing and the survey showed this was happening in a few cases. Even here one needs to consider carefully whether this is not a short-term expedient which will lead to later difficulties, particularly if other housekeeping operations are automated later and you need to be able to interrelate the data your existing database contains.

One of the main conclusions that Pat Manson[23] draws is about the growing use of specialist library software:

> What the past couple of years (1984-6) have seen above all has been the move away from in-house customization of general purpose software towards the growing market in dedicated library housekeeping systems software.

Cost
It still costs money after you have made the initial purchase.

There is a temptation when arguing your case for finance to start automating to concentrate on the one-off starting costs particularly the hardware, software and any associated stationery. You argue that either there will be a financial saving or a more efficient use of resources with automation. However there are other costs and these are of three kinds:

1 Processing and stock preparation
This is particularly true when installing issue systems because to operate the system your stock must be processed in advance. The biggest task is bar-coding your existing stock. Start bar-coding new additions to stock as soon as possible after deciding to automate even though your date for going public is some way off. It is far easier to incorporate bar-coding into normal book processing than to do it retrospectively from stock on the shelves. However you cannot escape dealing with existing stock on the shelves, almost certainly while the library is open. Unless you have considerable spare staff capacity (a most unlikely situation!) you could be faced with a near impossible task which might never be completed. It is essential to have manpower available to complete this task within your timetable. Apart from the operational need to get started it becomes a political embarassment if you don't appear to be delivering the goods.

There are two possible solutions, the first of which is for the college to redeploy other clerical staff or make available money to purchase temporary staff. Difficult in these days; if you are pursuing that route make sure that you have firm arrangements drawn and built into your timetable from the outset. At Edge Hill College we had a false start based on misleading information and although it was eventually resolved we lost several valuable months.

The second solution, and one which should be carefully investigated, is to arrange for your supplier to be responsible for the bar-coding and to include a sum of money within your initial capital sum for installation costs. There are all kinds of permutations as to how the responsibilities between yourself and the supplier may be worked out but it gets over the problem because it is a one-off operation and local authorities are much more ready to provide finance in this way than by increasing their staffing bill.

2 Service and maintenance

This can be expensive. Maintenance contracts on equipment are usually around 10% of the total purchase price and software support can be even more expensive. You need reliable arrangements and you must be prepared to pay for them. If you are using standard equipment it may be that the college or LEA has a more general service agreement which will cover you but make sure that it works quickly enough for you to maintain your service – sometime later in the week will not do! It may be cheaper and more efficient to buy additional equipment, an extra micro and screen and printer for example, and to pay for repairs as necessary than to take out expensive equipment contracts.

3 Upgrading: systems don't wear out, they just become obsolete!

The postscript to the Edge Hill story is a graphic example of what can be expected once you get into the automation process. Information technology is advancing at such a tremendous rate that any library using computer-based systems must be prepared to build in the cost of obsolescence. Fay[24] 'The need to replace obsolescent and decrepit equipment that cost so much so recently must be faced.' This may be a major upgrade of the system or new equipment, for example micros with extended storage capacity or a more efficient printer. This could happen every three or four years. Systems don't wear out, they just become obsolete! Perhaps it is more accurate to say that your library's needs change and the systems are constantly being developed that can respond to these needs by incorporating the latest advances in information technology.

People

You may be a leader in innovation in your college – but don't forget to take people with you.

Perhaps the last lesson is the most important. You may have an automated system but never forget it is operated by people for people. There are, we suggest, three groups to consider:

1 Library staff

These are the people at the sharp end who have got to implement and operate the system. Both professional and support staff work as a team and will have an interest in and concern about the new venture. They will have been subjected to the pressures which led to the need for change; they will want to know whether this development will really help to solve that problem. At different levels and in different ways they will be interested in and perhaps excited about taking part in something new, particularly as it appears to be part of an innovatory process which is taking place throughout our society and which they experience in so many facets of daily life. They are part of an organization that is 'with it', and that can be a great morale-booster.

They will also have concerns – perhaps anxieties. Novelty and excitement are one thing but how will it affect me? Will I be able to cope? Reducing routine tasks may be fine but what about the assistant who finds reassurance and security in that routine and for whom the new situation may appear threatening? Questions of job reduction or loss as a result of automation do not really apply in college libraries. Levels of staffing are such that any longer-term saving in staff time can be deployed to maintain and extend the service.

A programme of information, training and professional staff development must be worked out and implemented as part of the overall strategy. People are more likely to respond positively if they know what they have to do, why they are doing it, and where it fits in to the overall picture. For the middle management professional first-hand experience of this kind will be invaluable for their future career and they should be encouraged to relate what is happening in their own library to the broader professional scene.

2 College management

It is obvious that management will be involved initially with the proposal since it will require decisions about the deployment of college resources. If the librarian has developed his professional role and this is appreciated by the college management he will already have an accepted channel of communication. We have already discussed the specification: this will need to be appended to the case for automation and put to the management. While this may be the same document as that used with our third group, your library users, the emphasis will need to be different. It should be evident but it is not always recognized that users and management have different perspectives and you must take this into account. Management will want to know the contribution this project will make to the college, to evaluate the cost benefit compared with other possible developments. Your arguments need to be shaped accordingly, taking into account both long-term as well as more immediate benefits.

Given a reasonably responsive senior management it will pay dividends in the longer term if you update and inform the college managers of your progress. Don't assume that the principal or his deputy are clairvoyants: they will only know what is going on in the library if you take the trouble to tell them. If you wait for something to happen it is likely to be a crisis or at least something negative when the librarian is on the defensive.

Automation is positive and it is news. Capitalize on it!

3 The users

If automation is news to college management it is likely to be even more of a talking point among your users.

There will always be a vein of healthy scepticism among many lecturers about projects involving what to them will seem substantial amounts of expenditure in areas other than their own. There are two factors about a development of this kind, however, that make it unlikely that you will face that barrage of concerted cynicism that can be so wearing and discouraging. First, the pervasive nature of a central learning agency is usually well understood and expenditure here is not feeding a departmental or sectional ambition. Second, most lecturers will have some appreciation that since libraries deal with information the application of computer techniques is particularly appropriate. Students, on the other hand, may well be among your greatest supporters. They are likely to appreciate the potential benefits particularly from an automated issue system obviating the need to fill in slips and, hopefully, giving faster retrieval and more accurate information.

Information bulletins, demonstrations, regular updates of progress, all are important in maintaining effective channels of communication. Once your library has become involved with automation it has applied a technology which it will never discard. It may extend, upgrade or modify but the only way is forward, never back. Information technology is above all interactive, that approach should enhance all that is positive in the librarian's relationship with clients. A technology that enables us to re-evaluate and improve our relationship with our clients is fundamental to the success of the library.

As a footnote, it is interesting to compare the lessons learned at Edge Hill College with the points Peter Evans[25] makes in his article on the 'Management of an automation project'. Although he writes from a commercial point of view (he is the Managing Director, Biblio Tech Ltd, a firm of specialists in library computer systems) there is much common ground.

In-house production of documents

In addition to the more specialized library operations we have been considering there are those aspects of the electronic office which can profitably form part of the library's operations. If the library has automated its acquisitions then it is a logical step to handle its financial records using a spreadsheet. This may well be largely included in the acquisitions package. The use of electronic mail has already been mentioned. This may be part of a college information system. The most common use of microcomputers is for word-processing and while this can be used for general correspondence there are opportunities for either initiating or improving the library's document production.

If the college library functions effectively it will produce its own documents as well as receiving and managing materials. The means to produce information and guides about the system; abstracts; literature searches; bibliographies and bulletins about new additions has been made more possible by using the micro and printer with a wordprocessing package. The advent of desk-top publishing allows copy to be presented in an attractive and arresting way. If this is linked to a laser printer then the means of in-house production has been greatly extended. Even if the laser printer is not possible, just using a standard wordprocessing package with a straightforward printer allows for the production of satisfactory camera-ready copy. It also means that where you wish to update or cumulate material this is simple using information stored on disc in a way that was just not possible from typescript.

Into the fifth generation

Any account of future developments in information technology must make reference to the next major move forecast in computer technology. Commonly known as fifth-generation computer systems we are looking at computers that are different from their predecessors because they will have the power to reason. Fifth-generation computers will store huge amounts of information which they will be able to interpret, update and package. The user will be able to

127

communicate with them in everyday language and the computer will be able to respond with knowledge and information packaged for the individual's specific needs. These systems will be knowledge information processing systems with an 'intelligent' ability to process similar to humans. Central to fifth-generation computers is the development of artificial intelligence. These machines will be able to collect, assemble, select from, understand and perceive. They will be able to think like human beings, but unlike humans, they will not be able to appreciate the reason for and significance of their actions. This distinction needs to be made because of the discussion about 'Can computers think like human beings?' They will be extremely powerful and important tools but they will not have many of the necessary human attributes. Kilgour[26] says:

> Expert systems – or knowledge-based systems, as you say in England – are artificial intelligence programs. They have been defined as computer programs that perform at the level, or beyond the level, of expert human capabilities. The knowledge of knowledge-based systems is of two types. The first is conceptual and factual that pervades library materials of all kinds. The second is knowledge that may be unique to a single individual; it can be thought of as intuition, rule of thumb and effective guessing. These two types of knowledge, in combination with problems for simple problem-solving logic and application of common-sense reasoning, comprise knowledge-based systems.

Before considering the implications for libraries we must say something about applications to further education more generally. Following work on fifth-generation computing in America and Japan the UK government first commissioned a Report on Advanced Information Technology (the Alvey Report, 1982[27]) and followed this in 1983 with the establishment of a five-year collaborative research programme (the Alvey Programme). The Alvey Programme is based on collaboration between government departments (Trade & Industry, Education & Science and the Ministry of Defence); academic institutions and research groups; industrial companies.

The original Alvey Report referred to universities but made no reference to further education. Further education colleges with their experience in vocational education and their close links with local employers have a crucial role to play in two areas:

● Developing and extending computer literacy for the post-16s.
● Training in high-technology manpower to develop and, more particularly, to service fifth-generation computing.

The Alvey Programme is currently supporting work at Kingston

College of FE on a project 'Knowledge-based engineering training' in collaboration with the Engineering Industry Training Board, Logica (software house), Imperial College, London, and Exeter University. Another example of interest in intelligent systems comes from the Manpower Services Commission which is developing a suite of demonstration expert sytems and providing support for trainers in industry in the use of knowledge-based systems. The Information Technology Development Unit at Kingston College of FE is active in the field and its activities are describd by Richard Ennals[28] and also in the *Education* digest on 'Information technology: the fifth generation and FE'[29] which gives a useful background survey. These include cooperation with FEU[30] in both courses and publications about fifth-generation computers and the implications for FE. Ennals[31] points out that:

> the role of FE colleges in the future will be crucial . . . the reasons are simply that the FE sector is used to talking to industry and can respond to their training needs quickly; secondly FE staff seem to find it easier to talk to each other and to industry than university staff across many different subject departments.

Unfortunately it appears that currently the government is showing some reluctance to continue supporting this approach.

Implications for libraries
In this book we can only comment briefly. For a fuller consideration the latter half of Kilgour's *Beyond bibliography*,[32] will give much food for thought.

The significance of fifth-generation computers in the library cannot be under-estimated. It should lead to intelligent machines that make it possible for each user to ask for the specific information he requires. Furthermore it can be asked for in his own terms and at his own convenience. He will be able to call on large stores of information far beyond the confines of one institution.

> [it] will transform the traditional library, hitherto as inflexible and passive as the books and journals it contains, into the active, revolutionized library of the future.   Kilgour[33]

The implications for educational libraries and librarians are enormous. It gives a new imperative to the debate about the proactive/reactive role of the college library. It is crucial to the question of student-centred learning that we have discussed earlier.

The development of these systems and their introduction into further and higher education will require colleges to undertake a fundamental reappraisal of their approach to learning and the design of courses. It will have a great impact on teaching staffs and, in consequence, will require major staff-development programmes.

In this transformation of the nature of college education, for it will be no less, the role of the library will have to be reassessed in a more fundamental way than ever before. This reassessment will not necessarily be librarian-led. The impetus may well come from the college management, course-planning teams, or validating bodies. The question librarians have to ask of themselves is, can I respond?

The answer must be in the affirmative. Time does not stand still and when the challenge comes, for come it surely will, librarians who cannot go forward will find themselves pushed to one side. If the librarian cannot develop the library as the central college proactive knowledge-processing system based on fifth-generation computers then this function will be fulfilled in some other way. The library exists in name but it will become a backwater and an alternative organization will be developed. Eventually the official library dies or subsides into a custodial print collection while the dynamic of satisfying the institution's information needs and knowledge processing is transfered elsewhere. College libarians of the future may have a central role far greater than they occupy today, but they have to earn it and to show that they are capable of shouldering this extra responsibility.

References
1 Masterson, W., *Information technology and the role of the library*, Croom Helm, 1986.
2 'Databases for education', an *Education* digest, *Education,* 169, (8), 1987.
3 Information Technology Advisory Panel, 'Report', in *Education* digest, *Education,* 169, (8), 1987.
4 Taylor, J., 'Educational counselling and credit transfer service', *Learning Resources Journal,* 2, (3), LRDG, 1986, 125-36.
5 op. cit. 2.
6 Ramsden, A., 'Going on-line with a micro', *Library micromation news,* 11 January 1986, 4-9.
7 Ramsden, A., 'Going on-line with a micro', *Learning Resources Journal,* 2, (3), LRDG, 1986, 116-24.
8 op. cit. 6 and 7.
9 Lancaster, F.W., 'The future of the library in the age of telecommunications', in *Telecommunications and libraries,* NY Knowledge Industry Publications Inc., 1981, 137-56.

10 Lancaster, F. W., *et al.*, *The impact of the paperless society on the research library of the future,* University of Illinois, 1980.

11 Fay, D., 'Computing in further education: a personal philosophy', *Learning Resources Journal,* 3, (1), LRDG, 1987, 26-32.

12 op. cit. 4.

13 Roach, K., 'Interactive video and the curriculum', *Learning Resources Journal,* 3, (1), LRDG, 1987, 14-25.

14 Oldham, B., 'Interactive video: a realistic appraisal', *Learning Resources Journal,* 1, (1), LRDG, 1985, 19-25.

15 op. cit. 14.

16 Hammond, N., *Getting started: an introduction to microcomputers,* Getting Started Training, 53 High Street, Ramsbury, Wiltshire, SN88 2QN.

17 Steele, A., 'Interactive video in education: a trainer's view', *Learning Resources Journal,* 1, (2), LRDG, 1985, 4-8.

18 'Survey of microcomputer-based library automation member colleges', *LRDG Newsletter,* No. 5, October 1986, 4-5.

19 Burton, P., *Microcomputers in library and information services,* Gower, 1986.

20 Wilson, R., 'Library automation: an annotated bibliography', *LRDG Bulletin,* 11, July 1984, 15-25.

21 Manson, P., 'Library housekeeping systems for smaller libraries: an overview of trends in microcomputer-based systems', *Learning Resources Journal,* 2, (2), LRDG, 1986, 58-69.

22 op. cit. 18.

23 op. cit. 21, 66.

24 op. cit. 11, 32.

25 Evans, P., 'Management of an automation project: some guidelines', *Learning Resources Journal,* 1, (2), LRDG, 1985, 15-25.

26 Kilgour, F., 'Beyond bibliography', *Third British Library Annual Research Lecture,* British Library, 1985, 2.

27 Department of Industry, Alvey Committee, *Advanced information technology,* HMSO, 1982.

28 Ennals, R., 'Further education leadership for the fifth generation', *Education,* 168, (1), 1986.

29 'Information technology: the fifth generation and FE', *Education* digest, January 1986, *Education,* 167, (3), 1986.

30 Ennals, R., and Cotterell, A., *Fifth-generation computers: their implications for further education,* DES (FEU) 1985.

31 op. cit. 28, 11.

32 op. cit. 26.

33 op. cit. 26, 4.

Chapter 8   Libraries and learning resources

Introduction: what are learning resources?
In order to achieve a systematic approach to learning it is important to ensure the most efficient use of resources. To try and define those resources for learning immediately presents a difficulty; taken to its logical conclusion one may regard the whole college and everything in it, including the academic staff, as, directly or indirectly, a learning resource.

For the purposes of this chapter we shall adopt a pragmatic, working definition which identifies learning resources as those centralized facilities which support teaching and promote learning. Learning resources will include all or some of the following:

- College library
- Multi-media resource centre
- Educational development activities
- Audio-visual services
- Computer education courses
- Computer-assisted *and* computer-based learning
- Computer services
- College-automated information and electronic mail systems
- Photocopying
- Off-set litho and other print systems

This leads to two important questions:

1   Not all resources will be centralized. What is the balance and rationale for determining what is held centrally and what is departmentally based?

2   How is the balance struck between teaching support (reactive) and the promotion of learning (proactive)? More importantly, is this proactive role even recognized by the college let alone accepted?

Finally it is perhaps worth making the point that learning resources do not just come into existence when some form of umbrella organization is created. A college needs these facilities whether there is a unified approach or not. Institutions have to face the fact that information is increasing and its technology changing at an ever-increasing rate and this means that none of the agencies listed above can operate wholly in isolation. Educational technology embraces computer-assisted learning; libraries are computerizing both their information systems and housekeeping routines; the technology of interactive video involves both computing and technology; college printing will increasingly use desk-top/wordprocessing packages to create camera-ready copy; copies from this may be produced by laser printer rather than offset litho. The examples can be multiplied almost endlessly down to such practical considerations as, is it sensible to have two sets of technicians separately responsible for maintaining audio-visual equipment and computer hardware? Should not growing collections of computer software and video material be housed in a library/resource centre rather than build up separate organizations?

Expectations and objectives

All the links and overlaps we have just mentioned reinforce the case for a systematic approach to the provision of such facilities. Since the early 1970s many colleges have addressed themselves to this question. The motives were varied but chief among them were a more rational management structure which tackled the overlaps mentioned above; a more effective means of achieving the college's educational objectives; a more cost-effective use of resources that were becoming ever more varied and expensive during a period of increasing financial stringency.

What does college management expect of learning resources? McGettrick[1] lists five factors which lead to the effective management of an educational institution:

- Leadership of the institution.
- The climate of the institution ('ethos').
- The curriculum of the institution.
- Monitoring procedures in the institution.
- Expectations of the institution.

These have important 'messages' for the organization of learning resources because 'similar issues must affect the capacity of learning resources to demonstrate its effectiveness'. He goes on to discuss each of these factors in terms of learning resources. It is encouraging to find a college principal with such a clear grasp of the needs and such a positive approach. Taking the five headings above, McGettrick's expectations of learning resources can be summarized as:

Leadership

- Learning resources must be an 'integral and essential' part of the institution.
- Learning resources should be clearly related to the purpose of the institution.
- Learning resources provision should have an accepted place in the management of the institution and make its contribution to the policies of the institution.

There needs to be an attitude which appreciates that learning resources is 'not merely a marginalized assembling of materials but is a systematic ordering of information to be made accessible to those who require it. . . . Management therefore expects of learning resources the full participation in the development of academic policies.'

Climate

This not an easy concept to define. The learning environment has to be conducive to that purpose. It should be:

- Welcoming of the learner.
- Responsive to the needs of the learner.
- Professionally efficient and without needless bureaucratic constraints.
- Adaptive to the different learning styles of different people.
- Capable of adaptation and development to keep abreast of advances in new technologies.

The curriculum

The organization of learning resources must underpin the curriculum of the institution. College managements must recognize the importance of the close relationship between the curriculum and the resources supporting it. There are a number of expectations of management which should be highlighted in relation to the curriculum:

1 *The way in which students learn* – the 'process' rather than thinking purely in terms of content. The organization and use of learning resources will need to reflect this

2 *'Autonomy' in learning* – the importance of choice; the pace at which a student learns; aspects of open learning. These will require flexible and adaptive learning resources systems.

3 *The emphasis on learning and the centrality of learning resources* – this realization of the significance of learning resources has enabled educators to consider strategies for learning. New technology has

enabled information to be provided with an immediacy and a reality hitherto unknown.

4 *Monitoring* – the monitoring of the whole institution should include the provision and operation of its learning-resource organization. In addition to this management should recognize that through learning resources it is possible to work across the institution and to monitor certain practices which are part of the whole educational process. The three areas where this is most likely are:

- Course design
- Course delivery
- Management information

Expectation

McGettrick says that the expectations of management in learning resources must be 'realistic, and these are likely to be characterized by an openness to change and growth; a flexibility in meeting the differing needs of learners; and a responsiveness to the institutions and requests of management'.

Conversely failure by learning resources to participate in the institution as a whole can lead to features such as:

(a) A marginalized learning resources provision where it is seen as an optional extra
(b) An inflexible management of resources which does not meet the real needs of staff or students
(c) An organization of resources unable to respond to the pressures and changes which characterize education at present.

Responding to the challenge
What colleges need:

1 A clear decision to integrate/coordinate learning resources – who takes this? Is it management-led or arrived at by discussions and decision through the academic structures, i.e. academic board discussions?

2 A clear understanding as to how learning resources will fit into the college management structure. This means:

- Definition of the role of learning resources and its relationships with other organizational units within the college.
- Adjustment of those other units and the committee and information structure of the college to take account of this.

3 Consideration of how the provision of learning resources is going to be managed, in particular its leadership. What is the role of

the head of learning resources and what is his place in the management structure?

4   A belief in the value of learning resources and their contribution to learning – how will integration improve existing services and promote the growth of new areas? This should lead to a corporate identity and 'ethos' for learning resources.

5   Planning, development and research in learning resources – this can easily be overlooked or seen as something only appropriate to teaching departments. Attention needs to be given to:

- *The learning resources development plan* – which needs to be both distinctive and yet integrated with the college development plan. It needs a rolling programme for at least five years ahead to force people to think ahead and update their professional knowledge; to force them to consider the relevance of new developments to their own situation. In these days colleges cannot afford simply to be defensive, fighting localized rearguard actions. One must be positive, go out and face the world.

- *Staff development and research* – in learning resources this has a particular significance. In addition to the separate areas of technical and professional expertise of learning resources staff there is a need for *overall learning resources development.*

Both problems and opportunities occur particularly at the interface of the different learning resource operations. This may be simply modifying different organizational and operational patterns to enable different services to operate harmoniously together. More importantly it can mean re-education of staff and adjustment of attitudinal differences. The teacher in charge of a resource centre has a different approach to a librarian; the outlook of a technician, however skilled, is fundamentally different from the educational technologist. The computer specialist may have the greatest difficulty not only in relating to his other colleagues in their established roles but also in adjusting to the quite different needs of information technologist; computing tutor; software/hardware consultant/provider all implicit within his post. It is not too much to say that the success or failure of an integrated learning resources unit will in large part depend on the quality of staff development and the ability of the head of learning resources to get his senior staff working positively and constructively together.

6   A policy about centralized learning resources and departmental provision.

Better use of limited resources and better administrative control are arguments commonly put forward for centralizing learning resources. This may indeed be a result of integration and its administrative importance should not be underrated. However it is rather a limited objective and the reasons for developing learning resources should always be seen primarily in educational terms, enhancing the opportunities and the scope for learning. It is important to keep this in mind when trying to find the balance between centralized and department provision. Teaching departments will need to have resources which:

- Are particular to them.
- Need specialist professional/technical support often in a laboratory situation.
- Are necessary to support teaching and tutorial work in the departmental base.

Resources in centralized learning resources will be those which:

- Can be used by students and staff on different courses.
- Students need to use individually.
- Do not normally require the presence of the tutor/departmental technician.
- Need to be available in a controlled way for longer periods than is normally the case in teaching departments.
- Reinforce and extend teaching or promote individualized learning.

7   A means of asessing and evaluating learning resources.

Assessment and evaluation for the library has been dealt with in an earlier section, so it is sufficient to say here that qualitative as well as quantitative standards need to be monitored. The quality of learning resources needs to take into account the impact it has on student learning and the satisfaction level of its users as well as standards of provision. This is complex and difficult, going far beyond the transaction records usually kept by libraries and audio-visual services.

Two practical ways in which this monitoring can be achieved are:

- Setting up user groups for the various areas of learning resources and charging them (together with the staff concerned) with the responsibility of producing regular evaluations. These could include recommendations which, once agreed, would be acted on and monitored.
- Appointing an outside consultant. This person would have two functions, providing an external opinion on the general planning and direction of LR, even acting as a troubleshooter

if the need arose; giving an assessment of the services and facilities, usually in a written report.

There is a deficiency in published standards and criteria for assessment across the field of learning resources. Librarians have undertaken this task in respect of their service in works such as Shercliff's *College of education libraries research project*[2] now very much out of date, and the more recent Library Association COFHE Section standards[3]. The work of Kevin Donovan[4] has provided some useful approaches and we look forward with interest to the completion of the Learning Resources Development Group's research project on learning resource provision in colleges. The group appointed Gordon Brewer, then Head of Learning Resources, Bedford College of HE as research fellow and his report is expected during 1988. The survey covers some 60 colleges and the main outcomes are expected to be:

- Guidelines for the provision of learning resources services.
- Statistical evidence of the current range of services in colleges.
- Case studies illustrating the main organizational structures.
- A consultancy network for LRDG members.

For the first time this should provide information which will enable colleges to make assessments about learning resources against a norm and identify examples of good practice.

How do learning resources units work in practice?
A useful bank of case studies exists in an on-going series of articles in the *Learning Resources Journal*.[5] Each issue normally carries a case study of LR provision and development in one of its member colleges. During the last two years these have covered such diverse institutions as the Buckinghamshire College of HE; Cornwall College of F & HE; Tile Hill College of FE, Coventry; St Andrew's College of Education, Glasgow; South Bristol Technical College; Merchant Navy College. From these and the authors' own experience certain features emerge:

1   The initiative to centralize usually comes from within senior management.

2   The encouragement of senior management is essential since this is a centralized area of college activity.

3   The managerial and entrepreneurial qualities of the head of the learning resources organization are of prime importance to the success of the enterprise.

4   The management of people within learning resources units, the effective coordination of people with different outlooks and backgrounds, is one of the most difficult tasks the head of learning resources has to face.

5   College management having an overview of college affairs is likely to be more enthusiastic for learning resource development than teaching departments or individual lecturers.

6   The learning resources unit will need to demonstrate to college that there are positive benefits arising from its creation and that it was not just 'change for change's sake'.

7   Learning resources units will face particular challenges peculiar to them in effecting their educational role because they do not involve a predominant element of formal lecturing. They will have to devise strategies to allow this to be recognized in a situation where academic and educational work is accounted for on the basis of class teaching hours.

8   The contribution of learning resources to a student's development in the field of study skills, information handling, access to databases and other tools, familiarity with educational equipment, the interactive use of learning materials, and, in some cases, the ability to produce learning materials, is a life-long asset to the individual.

9   The environment of learning and assistance to the habit and enjoyment of learning is less tangible but in many ways as important as the provision of information and materials.

10   Of great practical advantage to a learning resources unit is the fact that it is charged with handling a large proportion of the college's annual revenue budget. This is power which creates opportunities but also carries responsibilities. It needs to be exercised with care.

11   The nature and ethos of the learning resources unit can vary in different institutions. The balance between the different sections can vary. So too can the balance between teaching, consultancy and service provision.

12   Most learning resource units cover library and audio-visual services. There is considerable variation in the inclusion of other aspects. The two most debated areas are printing and reprographics and computing. The latter is becoming a major question in college organization and is fundamental to future learning resources development.

13   Where a learning resources unit is established and working developmentally it becomes a powerful 'change agent' in the institution. It will promote awareness in college of the learning

potential of developments in information technology and the increasing interrelation of the materials and facilities in those areas of LR which had previously been separate.

14 Institutional change is usually greeted with scepticism in some areas of the college. This is certainly true when centralizing learning resources. However, once the organization is set up and seen to work it is there to stay. It would be a short-sighted college management that contemplated discarding the organization once it had been established.

The librarian and learning resources
In this section we address two questions: (1) What challenges face the librarian who becomes a head of learning resources? (2) How should the librarian respond if the library service becomes part of an integrated LR system?

The librarian who becomes head of learning resources
This section, written by Peter Pack, is based largely on his experiences as head of learning resources in a college of HE. The following points are those which on reflection seem to be of particular relevance. They will often reflect what has been said earlier in this chapter. The fact that they are raised should not be taken to mean that they were satisfactorily resolved or even fully realized during my time at the college. I had been a school librarian, a lecturer in a college of FE and a college of education tutor-librarian before becoming Head of Learning Resources at Edge Hill College in 1974. The main effects of this translation to a wider responsibility during the ten years I held that post were:

1 An immediate awareness of the 'difference' on accepting the post without fully appreciating what these differences were. It is easy to be wise in retrospect but those were pioneering days and one learnt by experience, often by one's mistakes!

2 The need to have a strategy for dealing with the fact that you were responsible for areas of college activity where you had staff with different qualifications and experience. This has to be tackled by personal staff development, seeking to gain understanding of the 'other area(s)'. One may take courses in educational technology leading to a qualification. This now includes qualifications and courses in computing. Alternatively one can deepen one's understanding of these other areas by discussion with specialists in those areas and by taking short courses without necessarily trying to

become qualified in each field. Over time I came to realize that, important as this background knowledge was, one's main function was management and it was of the greatest importance to develop management skills. My advice to anyone faced with this situation would be to concentrate on this area and if a formal qualification seemed appropriate then a post-graduate qualification in academic management would be my priority.

3   The need to be able to deal with the various levels of academic management in the college. If you are included (as I was) in the senior management team then you need to be able to operate at more than one level. You need to have a clear idea of the purpose and contribution of learning resources and to relate this to the matter under discussion. At the same time you need to be able to stand back and take a broader 'college' view. It is also important to be able to try and see the college's position in relation to national trends in further and higher education. In this latter context I was extremely fortunate to have undertaken a considerable amount of consultancy outside the college, in particular as a specialist adviser and Board Member of CNAA. I was encouraged to do so by my director and I owe him a debt of gratitude for this although I hope it was in large part repaid by the broader understanding I was able to bring to discussions in college at a period of development and change.

4   Learning to keep one's head above water and maintain a sense of proportion. As your range of responsibilities becomes wider so the pressures increase. It is essential that you maintain a sense of proportion. One way is to make sure that you have a regular 'escape route'. One of the values of my extra-mural activities with CNAA and other professional bodies was to achieve this. It isn't always appreciated or understood in the college, even by colleagues in learning resources. Stand firm. If you get the opportunity take it, and, provided you keep it in proportion, you, learning resources, and the college will all benefit.

5   The ability to delegate. This is another part of keeping your head above water. Don't try to hold on to the job you were doing as well as tackling the new one. The college has to realize that a learning resources unit is not just the library with other services tacked on. Establishing that is not easy and if you go on trying to be the college librarian it is well nigh impossible. It is also frustrating and limiting to your senior library staff. Your promotion to head of learning resources should offer something to them as well.

The converse of the librarian not being sufficiently self-confident to let go of his previous responsibilities is the college management that expects the former librarian to do two jobs. To be fair, this may be a matter of expediency since the college may not be able to make an additional appointment even though the need for this is recognized, but it does lead to difficulties. The recognition by college that the learning resources unit has a distinctive role is made that much more difficult. You can find situations when, as head of learning resources you have to make judgements, often on employing resources, between the different sections of your unit. You try to be objective but can your colleagues really believe in your objectivity? The twin dangers are either to over compensate or indulge in over-detailed self justification.

At Edge Hill we had something of this difficulty since we never formally appointed a head of library services, but I was fortunate in having academic library staff to whom I was able to delegate the day-to-day running of the library. In matters of resource deployment the senior staff of the unit, who met regularly as a team, discussed matters fully and openly. Over time we built up a framework of understanding in which these decisions were taken on a genuine unit basis with the interests of college in mind.

6 Forming a management team in learning resources. If your unit is to have any hope of success you must have your senior managers working together. That does not mean that they will always agree. It would probably be a rather bland and mediocre organization if they did. Problems occur within the sections of learning resources units but these should be solved by the managers of those sections. You may become involved if the matter is sufficiently serious but you will be working with and supporting the manager concerned. The problems in your management team will be largely those that occur at the interfaces between sections. They may be tangible and quantifiable or attitudinal, or a mixture of both.

It is essential that you have a framework in which matters can be thrashed out. If you don't face up to this you just store up trouble for the future. It is worth spending time talking things through: decisions arrived at after long and sometimes difficult discussions are more likely to be accepted and applied wholeheartedly. It is also worth remembering that meetings of this kind gradually build up a mutual appreciation of other people's point of view. They also develop a corporate identity among the team. At Edge Hill the learning resource managers met at least twice per term with more meetings if necessary. A written record was kept of meetings, decisions made and action to be taken. These decisions and action were reviewed at subsequent meetings.

7   Finally a word about staff development. The librarian is well aware of the importance of this. As head of learning resources the responsibility becomes that much more complex. Staff appraisal is currently a much-discussed topic and it may be that institutions now practise this as part of their college policy. One of my last innovations at Edge Hill was to introduce a regular system of staff development interviews for professional and technical learning resources staff. It was at an early stage when I left but at that time we were pioneering.

The librarian as part of the learning resources unit

If a librarian is appointed to run the library services after the unit has been formed then he accepts the organization which he has joined. However there are many colleges where librarians who were formerly in charge of a separate service now are responsible to a head of department or college manager with different qualifications and experience from their own. The following remarks are comments on this situation.

We all value our independence. Whatever part we play within an organization we like to feel that there is something for which we are responsible. Put another way we want to believe that if we were absent for whatever reason we would be missed. This is perfectly natural and in no way conflicts with our institutional or professional loyalties or our wish and ability to cooperate with others. If somebody has been responsible to the head of an institution for an area of that institution's activity it requires a major readjustment of attitude to come to terms with being part of a larger organization and working to a new head.

The major problems are likely to be:

1   Loss of status – not salaried position, but the less tangible regard in which one is held by the college and in particular one's own library staff. Allied to this can be the feeling that not only you but the library has been diminished in the eyes of the college.

2   Inability to have a direct line of communication with the principal. You may not have used it frequently in the past but it was comforting to know it was there. Now you have to go to somebody else.

3   The need to attend more meetings and discuss what you previously 'just got on and did'.

4   Finding that your area of independent action is more limited.

5   Being required to have an understanding of related learning resource areas that you previously didn't think about because they were somebody else's concern.

6 Trying to explain your point of view to somebody whose background and outlook is different. To suggest that the outlook of college librarians is insular and introverted would be both an overstatement and an unfair generalization. However an established and experienced college librarian develops a particular professional point of view and it can come as something of a shock to have to explain, and in some cases justify, what has been taken for granted. For example the librarian's apparent obsessiveness with security might be seen as unduly negative. However the librarian knows, often from bitter experience, that the most imaginative and worthwhile schemes to develop facilities for study and learning can be seriously impaired by the loss of the vital piece of study material when it is required. Having to argue this point seems time-consuming and wearing.

These are real concerns: they will exist whether or not they are articulated, and the head of the unit will need to give them serious attention when considering his management strategies and staff development programme. The following comments try to emphasize the more positive aspects:

1 Having a head of department to deal with rather than going direct to the principal allows more immediate and frequent access.
2 The head of learning resources will have a senior status and be able to advance the case of the library along with the other parts of the unit in policy and resource discussions.
3 The head of learning resources may not have your particular professional understandings but he will be sympathetic to library provision as part of learning resource development. As head of the unit he has a direct responsibility for each of its sections and an interest in seeing them perform well.
4 Having to work as part of a team brings the librarian into contact with education technologists, managers of audio-visual services, information technologists and others in a way that would otherwise be unlikely to happen. Having to work together gives new insights and understanding of related areas.
5 Having to face the challenge of a new situation may be just what was needed to get the librarian and the library service out of a rut. Painful initially, but in the longer term recognized as well worthwhile!

The future of learning resources services
As we indicated at the start of this chapter there are many different

types of learning resource organization and this is exemplified by the case studies in the *Learning Resources Journal.* In the rapidly changing world of information technology it is unlikely that any organization will remain static. In some cases the increasingly complex interaction of the different components of learning resources services will lead to an ever more closely knit unit. Perhaps the changing technology and evolving patterns of learning needs will lead to substantial modification of traditional groupings such as the library; educational technology; audio-visual services and computing. We may see them replaced with such facilities as independent learning centres, automated and electronic information services, self-learning materials production centres alongside banks of hardware and multimedia materials for loan.

The alternative is also possible, particularly in larger colleges where the increasing range and complexity of learning facilities leads to a looser form of association. The various parts of learning resources services are coordinated at senior management level but they operate as largely independent entities with cooperation at various levels as the need arises. Whichever route a college follows, the relationship of the various learning resource agencies and their effect on student learning will be of major and increasing significance in the years ahead.

References

1   McGettrick, B., 'What management expects of learning resources', *Learning Resources Journal,* 2, (3), LRDG, 1986, 92-100.

2   Department of Education and Science, *College of education libraries research project,* (Project Director Shercliff), HMSO, 1972.

3   Library Association, *Colleges of further and higher education: guidelines for professional services and resources provision,* 3rd edn, Library Association, 1982.

4   Donovan, K., *Learning resources in colleges: their organization and management,* CET, 1981.

5   *Learning Resources Journal,* 1, (2), to 3, (2), LRDG, 1985-87.

Chapter 9   Thoughts about college librarians

The purpose of this chapter is to set down some thoughts about the professionals who manage or work in college libraries. Throughout we have been concerned with resources and our greatest resource is the human resource: the librarian and his professional colleagues.

The identity of the college librarian
The profession of the librarian was established by Royal Charter. Whatever terms were set down the living definition of a profession is determined by the operations of its members and the perception of those operations by its clients and the community at large. There are large national and local authority libraries that are general in nature and it is probably true to say public awareness of and attitudes to libraries and librarians are conditioned by experience of the public library. It is also true that there is seldom any distinction in the public's mind between the professional librarian and the library assistant. Indeed the common image of the librarian is either the assistant carrying out a loan transaction or the introvert and rather formidable creature who insists on silence! Stereotypes exist for all professions but librarians are particularly badly served in this respect. It is a point that can have its effect on the perception of the college librarian by the college staff and students.

Although there are general libraries, the library profession is by and large a federal profession. As such, it has certain features which have to be recognized and come to terms with. Librarians work in many specialized contexts, often being alone or part of a small section within a much larger concern. As a result they often take on the corporate identity of their employers as well as retaining their individual professional identity. This duality can have a number of effects. First, it can enrich the background and outlook of the individual. Because he is relating a professional skill to a particular context there is an area of activity and knowledge that he is exploring with a sense of purpose. Interpersonal contacts can be fruitful and constructive with benefits to all concerned in contributing to a common goal.

146

Second, librarians are 'different'. In a college the most cohesive professional group is the teaching staff. They are the most expensive resource in terms of the annual revenue budget. Their professional activity is central to the purpose of the institution. Many other people are employed in the college in a variety of occupations but they are seen as support or ancillary, whether assisting teaching or in administrative or domestic roles. However, the role of the library is fundamental both to support teaching and to promote learning. Some of the more obvious technical and clerical routines are clearly supportive but the senior levels of operation, consultancy, information services, user education and training, together with the leadership and managerial role of the librarian are of a scale and level that requires appropriate recognition within the academic structure of the college. It should not be forgotten that many college librarians are at least as well qualified both academically and professionally as their colleagues on the teaching staff. But what is the appropriate recognition?

One aspect of not being quite sure where one stands is the sense of loneliness that can be felt by college librarians, particularly in smaller colleges. We are talking of professional isolation; on a personal level they may have many friends but they have no peer or mentor to whom they can turn. Equally there is seldom any inspector or adviser to assist them. Earlier we have dealt with the library's educational role but the different nature of the library operation and the different background and experience that librarians normally have from lecturing staff means that for the librarian there is an intangible but real barrier.

The remainder of this chapter deals with the relationship with the principal; thoughts on salaries and conditions of service and, finally, aspects of staff development and training. All of these relate to identity, finding oneself professionally.

The librarian and the principal
In Chapter 8 ('Libraries and learning resources') we pointed out that the librarian may no longer be directly responsible to the head of the institution. For principal you may have to substitute that member of senior management who has responsibility for the library. Equally we may be talking of the relationship of the head of learning resources to the principal. Whatever the precise situation, the general point remains: the relationship between the head of the library service and the person representing the senior management of college is critical to the success of that service. We emphasize the relationship between

people here. This is not to diminish or disregard the importance of being able to work effectively through college committee structures presenting well documented cases and arguing cogently. However, this is a relationship between managers, both of whom have been appointed to run a particular organization.

This chapter is about identity. While we are considering the relationship with the principal it is worth remembering the parallel we have already drawn between the college as an institution and the library, as a sub-system within a system. Although the library is an integral part of the college it is also an entity. While the same may be true of subject departments (their autonomy varies according to the management structure of the college) the library is different in nature and its remit is college-wide. It provides for all students and staff; its finances, both revenue and capital, are provided for the whole institution. It has senior staff with distinctive professional qualifications (by this we mean that qualified librarians are almost certainly going to be the largest group of professionals other than the teaching staff). It is housed in separate accommodation (we are not necessarily implying physically separate or purpose-built but permanently designated for library use and developed as such). If the institutional environment is being evaluated the library can be a major criterion by which the academic health of that institution is judged. This is certainly true in the case of institutional reviews undertaken by the Council for National Academic Awards.

The librarian is head of this institution. He is the manager. Many of the attitudes and approaches he must adopt if he is doing his job effectively will be recognized and appreciated by the principal. The principal and librarian are both managers and there can be an immediate level of understanding of each other's methods and problems. This understanding may also exist between the principal and the heads of major teaching departments but the librarian has an additional link. Heads of departments have a sectional interest and they will on occasion have to balance college needs against the interests of their departments. The librarian, because of his central role as manager of a college-wide service, experiences to a degree the responsibility of listening to the evidence and making judgements as to how best to deploy his limited resources among many competing interests. This is an experience he shares with the principal and other senior members of the college management.

The librarian's managerial understanding is potentially of enormous value to him in his relations with the principal. Where it is not recognized and used to develop a rapport, this may be due to the principal taking a more limited view of the library, in which case the librarian has an uphill task. It may be, however, that the reason lies with the librarian. Perhaps he is not a sufficiently effective manager to think of himself in these terms. Perhaps the librarian has simply never considered it in this way in which case it would be greatly to his, the library's, and ultimately the college's benefit if he undertook an urgent reappraisal of his role.

Notwithstanding the many constraints both internal and external that operate on the college, the principal exercises a considerable amount of power. He also is subject to and responds to pressures. He is a busy person, usually working at several levels simultaneously, dealing with such matters as external relations, policy, college development, financial constraints, pressures from validating bodies. At the same time he must be sensitive to day-to-day happenings in college. Most of the running of college may have been delegated, but the finger must be kept on the pulse and he fails to do this at his peril.

Principals are not polymaths. They are often unaware of much of the detail of whole areas of college work. This is not a criticism, for no single person could encompass this range except in the small specialist college and even there it is likely that the latest advances in the subject are absorbed by teachers and research staff rather than the principal. It means that different areas of the college are seen by the principal in relation to his overall college management strategy, and his perception of the role each part has in that strategy is determined either by his preconceptions or by the understanding he has been given by the person in charge of that area.

How should the librarian relate to the principal?
While there can be no blueprint, some points are worth remembering:

1   Get to know as much as you can about the person, particularly about his professional interests. Obviously you want to know about his attitude to the library service but don't be too narrow in your approach. He is likely to be a complex personality; it is important to study his manner and style of operation. Is he willing to learn or 'big' enough to listen to others? Is he competent but pedestrian or has he a real talent for the job, that extra flair which can be sensed rather than defined?

2   Is he your sort of person? If you are able to manage and assess people, which as a librarian you certainly ought to be, then you should soon know whether you can establish a rapport which will be the basis for a constructive professional dialogue. This may sound obvious but there are occasions when the chemistry isn't right.

Neither person is unprofessional but communication is an effort to be indulged in as little as possible.

3   Have you kept him informed? The principal will only know about your library if you tell him. Otherwise he only has his own observations, hunches and preconceptions. The chances are that the library will never impinge on his consciousness from one set of revenue estimates to the next unless you do something about it. Of course something may crop up which is not to your choosing, such as a dispute with a course leader or subject department over demands made on the library, or unrest by the students' union over opening hours. In cases like these the librarian is almost always on the defensive and the impression given of the library is negative. So take the initiative: keep him up to date with the positive things the library does, developments in services, publications, staff development activities, increases in turnover. He may not read it all in detail or even appreciate the finer professional points (best to keep it concise with precis and abstracts attached) but it will keep the library in his mind and help to build up a positive impression.

Salaries and conditions of service
Salaries and conditions of service of librarians are usually held to be the practical demonstration of the library's standing in the college. As such they are a powerful aid to establishing identity. Are they paid on Burnham or local government salary scales? Have they got teaching conditions of service or is it a hybrid post? How many tutor-librarians are there? In addition there is also the matter of grade or level of renumeration. These questions indicate real uncertainties and difficulties, not only on the part of librarians but also principals and others responsible for determining posts and making appointments.

We said earlier in this chapter that librarianship is a federal profession and that librarians often take on the corporate identity of their employers. In many types of institution the salary structure and conditions of service present no difficulty other than determining the level of remuneration relative to other employees. In higher and further education the lecturers scales are meant for those who *teach* and are bureaucratically determined in terms of class contact hours. The exception is the head of department scale. The college has first to decide that its library is of sufficient importance for the librarian to be designated a head of department. Such a post then has to be found within the establishment. Since the number of heads of department, and their grading, depends on the size and level of work in the college, the use of one such post for the librarian may mean that difficult decisions have to be made.

Salaries and conditions of employment for lecturing staff
Different inputs need to be made within the college to create
conditions where effective learning can take place. The present
conditions for employing college staff do not assist this. There is an
absolute division between 'teaching' and 'non-teaching' staff, a
polarization which is unrealistic and almost certainly leads to
difficulties in management. There are a number of posts in college
which are not covered by a rigid insistence on the class teaching hours
criteria. Careers counsellors, educational technologists, computing
staff with responsibilities for management as well as skills teaching,
are all categories who to some degree find what they do at variance
with their conditions of employment. Then there are the levels of
college management. One accepts that this has been catered for in the
senior posts of principal, deputy principal and heads of department,
but if courses are to run effectively there must be a great deal of
delegated management which is grafted on to the more senior
teaching posts. There is also the whole time-consuming area of
student counselling, covering social and personal as well as matters of
educational performance.

The conditions of employment for lecturers still emphasize the
class teaching aspect of their activity when this is becoming a less
significant element of their contribution to student learning. Indeed
the salary award to FE lecturers increases the limit of teaching hours
to a maximum of 21 hours per week.

As we outlined in Chapter 4 ('Educational technology and
educational objectives') there are alternatives to a teacher-led,
lecture-based approach. Our professional analysis of what stimulates
effective learning together with developments in the technology of
information and education has given us the opportunity to make
improvements in the way we educate students. But how can we move
to a more flexible, student-centred approach within the straitjacket of
the existing conditions of service? First there must be the will for
change on the part of the lecturing staff. This would never be easy to
achieve and it will be particularly difficult at this time of stress in
higher and further education. The instinct of human beings to protect
themselves and survive is as powerful in present-day professions and
institutions as it was for our forbears in the primeval jungle. We
rationalize away from our immediate situation into the more general,
distant, impersonal and safer. To reform the basis on which we
employ teaching staff in colleges is simply too radical, too personal
and too painful.

Yet to fail to do this and not to take institutional, profession-led,

151

initiatives to develop the quality of learning is to diminish the education profession's standing and credibility. It surrenders the initiative and this has allowed a reformist government to make the running, setting its own goals. It also isolates lecturers in the eyes of the public as cosy, comfortable and self-seeking.

We can look forward to further education in the future which has an emphasis on vocational suitability and industrial training. It will be a more uniform, conformist system, centre-led, with less freedom of action for the individual college, producing a more compliant student product. Conversely we can expect a diminution of opportunity for individuality, creativity and dissent. It is not suggested that these alternatives should be seen simply as good or bad, black or white. Rather that this trend is the result of educationalists failing to face up to the issues which involve radical professional change.

Meanwhile the government has not been idle. The tightening of the conditions of service mentioned above is but one aspect of the increasing centralization and control. Much more fundamental is the new government White Paper *Higher education: meeting the challenge,*[1] which proposes to remove almost all higher education from local authority control. Paragraph 4.47 of that report makes brief reference to academic pay, citing the work of the Croham Report. It indicates that the government will shortly start examining university pay and conditions and will at the same time 'be considering what arrangements should be adapted in the polytechnics and colleges sector'.

There is therefore the real possibility of different arrangements for pay and conditions of service in higher as opposed to further education. But is this an opportunity for attempting a radical alternative and, if so, what? We have taken this opportunity to make some suggestions of our own and then to consider the implications of what we are saying for librarians in colleges.

Thoughts about an alternative approach to pay in higher and further education

It should be perfectly possible to find ways of employing educational professionals in a more professional way. We have said earlier that teachers are not the only trained personnel required for learning in further education and that teachers themselves perform a number of tasks including formal classroom lecturing. It should be possible to allow educationalists to charge for their services, to work out categories of work and rates of renumeration for those categories. It is not suggested that we should go so far as to make teachers self-employed, but they should be employed on contracts which give a basic retainer and then specify the types of work the individual is to undertake, the proportion of the whole each activity will be and the rates of payment for the different activities. These contracts would either be fixed-term and renewable or – and this seems more likely to build confidence – permanent but with regular periods of updating and assessment built in. There should also be opportunities built in for rewards for performance above the norm or for additional responsibilities undertaken.

Salaries are only half the question: Conditions of service are as, or perhaps even more, important. It should be possible to specify basic leave periods which accord more nearly to the holidays taken by other professions. In addition to this there should be specified periods for preparation, research and staff development. No conscientious, hard-working professional should have anything to fear from this type of approach.

Such a system could, we believe, help to revitalize our colleges. It would reward initiative and enthusiasm; would promote real staff development; enable regular and effective monitoring of perform-ance. Colleges would be able to demonstrate to the world at large that their workforce was dedicated and fully committed. Those who at present give unstintingly way beyond what is formally required of them could reasonably expect some recognition of their endeavours. Those who did not fully pull their weight would face regular assessment when appropriate action could be taken.

Implications of this approach for librarians in colleges

1   The question of whether librarians are part of the teaching staff disappears. The nonsense of 'hybrid' posts would be a thing of the past. As a professional working in education you would be entitled to remuneration on the appropriate scales.

2   Any professional job, whether the head of the service or one of the professional staff, would be analysed and broken down into its major constituents. For librarians these could include: management and planning; consultancy; skills teaching; staff supervision; techni-cal operations (the word 'technical' is used in the broad sense to denote the performing of library tasks, e.g. classification, cata-loguing, inter-library loan procedures, which some professional librarians may undertake as part of their duties).

3   For each of these tasks there would be an agreed level of remuneration based on the nature of the task and the size and nature

of the institution. For example in a large college with a high proportion of advanced-level work there will probably be a number of professional staff. Among these staff there may be cases where only one type of work is undertaken by a member of staff (or predominantly so). In such a case the salary would be determined by the rate for that category together with a weighting for the responsibilities of providing for a large college and/or the advanced level of its work. On the other hand, in a small college with only one or two professional staff the range of tasks they perform will be much wider covering the whole spectrum of the library operation. For these people the equation will be more complex, but in many respects the analysis will be more valuable. The value will not just be in determining the level of salary, since it will demonstrate to the college management, in an objective way, just what one person is required to do in order to run a college library.

For librarians in smaller FE colleges there will probably need to be some kind of balancing factor if they are not to be treated unfairly, since neither size of institution nor the amount of advanced level work is likely to apply. This would need to give recognition to the range of responsibilities undertaken by one person since this requires exceptional self-discipline, self-organization and dedication to the job.

Staff development for librarians

The importance of staff development in colleges has been referred to at various points. In the fast-changing world of further and higher education staff at all levels, both teaching and non-teaching, need education and training to cope with change.

Staff development will affect the librarian in three ways:

- As part of general college staff development programmes designed to update and inform about higher and further education.
- As a provider of materials and facilities for other, more specialist, staff development programmes.
- Through staff development activities in the field of college librarianship.

It is this last category of staff development for librarians that concerns us and we end this final chapter with a consideration of some of the current issues.

If the service is to be maintained in a changing world, if it is to adopt new methods and techniques, and if it is to take on new tasks, then employers must invest in continuing education for their staff.

Employers must recognize that effective library and information services will depend on the quality of the professional staff running those services. If the service is to be efficient, up-to-date and able to meet changing demands imposed upon it, then staff must have adequate provision (funding and time) to maintain, develop and extend their professional skills.

UGC/NAB[2]

The report of the Transbinary Group on Librarianship and Information Studies charged with advising on and reviewing 'current provision and likely needs for library and information courses, likely future demand in terms of numbers and expertise for library and information professions' is important in connection with our attempts to review future trends in college librarianship for two basic reasons. Firstly, as is to a degree self-evident and to a degree argued within our thesis, the likelihood of achieving those aims, objectives and approaches we have been advocating, will be very much affected by the attitudes and types of personnel that are attracted in the first instance to undertake the profession of college librarianship. Secondly, college librarianship will be very dependent for its future successes on the level of commitment that can be secured for continuing education throughout the whole service.

The group's recommendations in both these areas make a good starting point. Both are encapsulated in the passages quoted. The emphasis on initial recruitment, the need for training relevant to current professional needs (e.g. a greater emphasis on science, technology, business, finance, law), recommendations about the unit of resource in UGC and NAB terms which library and information studies should attract and the pressures that should be put on funding bodies for increased resources for continuing education are all matters which college library managers support.

In the real world, however, we know that developments will not come quickly enough nor in sufficient degree. Prytherch[3] in his recent view on staff training in libraries paints a gloomy and piecemeal picture. Practitioners must be prepared to take their own steps to achieve more and better staff development. There are many positive ways in which college librarians can help their own cause.

Ours are very diverse types of institution both in terms of actual size and in variety of provision. Advantages and disadvantages come as an intrinsic part of whichever type or size of system might be one's particular concern. Those working in small organizations, for example, have opportunities for experiencing a wider range and variety of jobs, broadening their own expertise and possible job satisfaction. Set against this however are feelings of professional isolation that can come from having no professional peer group to relate to and to discuss issues with, together with the reduction of opportunities for leave to attend meetings, courses and conferences. Larger organizations will usually have more in-house opportunities for committee involvement, courses of study, larger budgets (but also more demands on them) for staff development programmes but day-to-day work for individual staff members is likely to be confined within narrower areas.

The problem of gradings for library staff features in this area of management in that regulations and funding governing release and payment of fees differ according to whether staff are on Burnham or NJC conditions of service. College library managers can be faced with the difficulty of explaining to members of their staff why it is possible to get approval for one and not for another – perhaps even to attend the same course.

Despite the problems, staff development remains a crucial part of a library manager's area of responsibility and never more so than at present:

> Being up-to-date with academic methods, with modern teaching strategies, with technological developments and with current practices in librarianship . . . the importance of this activity (i.e. staff development) cannot be overemphasized, since the up-to-dateness of the knowledge of the librarians, their level of motivation, both in terms of their own profession and the literature of the subjects taught in their institution, greatly affects the credibility and quality of the service that they are providing.
>
> Harrison[4]

It is generally the case that staff who have kept up-to-date are more confident and consequently more motivated, able and dynamic in their approach to the job and thus make a more effective contribution to the service.

Perhaps the best and first thing that the library manager can do is to create the atmosphere and dynamism that brings out qualities and aspirations of this sort in his staff.

Factors that will contribute to this include:

● Due attention to interview and selection procedures so that the right 'material' is selected initially.

156

- Staffing policies that deal fairly and positively with any existing staffing problems.
- Allocations of tasks that will 'stretch' less confident and less motivated staff members.
- Staff appraisal programmes.
- Efforts for staff in terms of effectively arguing cases with college management for regradings and promotions.
- Attention in positive rather than token terms to the requirements of staff in process of training.
- Availability of a good selection of professional literature and an encouragement to staff to read it and to discuss issues.
- A liberal attitude towards allowing time off for staff to get involved in professional meetings (e.g. CoFHE circles) – which are usually local and not subject to formal application procedures.

Many of these items have implications for the college librarian's own staff development requirements in terms of management skills.

Where college librarians are able to secure approval and funding for participation in more formal staff development exercises there is a wide variety of choice which can be used according to need, availability of time and funding. An examination of coming events and calendar sections of many professional publications will give some indication of the range and subject coverage. In addition, an examination of local college prospectuses can prove a fruitful source for things near at hand and covering the wider professional spectrum – e.g. educational technology, audio-visual, computing, statistics, finance, management – all of which are relevant for college library staff.

Examples of some of those available:

- Further education staff college courses.
- Short courses, conferences and workshops of such organizations as ACUCHE, ASLIB, NCET, LA, LRDG, NATFHE Library Section.
- Courses leading to higher degrees in one's own or neighbouring institutions.

Many commercial organizations are keen to demonstrate equipment and this can prove a useful source for gaining information in such areas for example as on-line systems, automation packages, computer software. These are also featured on occasions as part of the advertising section in professional conferences.

We have stressed at some length the need for user education and induction programmes for library clientele. The need for new library staff to be given appropriate induction courses and for all staff to be instructed when new equipment or processes are introduced should not be overlooked – an elementary but necessary part of staff development and continuing education.

References

1   Department of Education and Science, *Higher education: meeting the challenge*, Cm 114, HMSO, 1987.
2   University Grants Committee/National Advisory Body, *Report of the transbinary group on librarianship and information studies*, June 1986, British Library, 88 and 93.
3   Prytherch, R., *Staff training in libraries: the British experience*, vol. 1., Gower, 1986.
4   Harrison, C., 'Colleges and institutes of HE', in McElroy, A.R., (ed.), *College librarianship: the objectives and practice*, Library Association, 1984, 136-7.

In conclusion

Towards the 21st century: college libraries and the future
What will the college librarian face in the year 2000? It will be within
the working lifetime of many librarians now in colleges. How many of
them will still be there? How many will be doing something
completely different? Will they be self-employed, offering their talents
and experience outside the accepted patterns of professional employment?

This book started by looking to the immediate past to set the scene.
It considered the pressures and difficulties of college management in
present times but it has concentrated on the issues in college
librarianship that look forward.

In these closing passages we summarize some of the influences that
will affect colleges and their libraries in the years ahead.

General

- Changing social/economic patterns.
- Governmental policy and attitude.
- Changing balance of central/local government control.
- Greater input from commerce and industry.
- Impact of information technology.

This will lead to the following:

Colleges – general and management

- Modified roles for some colleges.
- Enhanced roles for outside agencies – e.g. MSC, Open College.
- Changed emphasis and significance in college governance.
- Different patterns of funding, a greater emphasis on alterna-
  tive sources of income.
- Greater emphasis on competition and marketing courses.
- Changes in forms of renumeration and conditions of service
  for teaching staff.

- Development of management information systems.
- Evaluation of management practice.
- More regular and systematic staff appraisal.

Teaching and learning
- More radical strategies to keep up with the increasing pace of the development of knowledge.
- More variety in age and course requirements of students.
- Greater use of the opportunities presented by information technology, particularly interactive technology.
- Greater flexibility in approaches to learning.
- More emphasis on open and distance learning.

Libraries
- An increased and more complex pattern of demand.
- Continuing stringency in resource provision.
- Greater diversity of types of material and associated hardware.
- A shift of emphasis from service provision based on a collection of materials to becoming an access point through which clients can acquire information.
- Greater coordination with other learning resource agencies within college.

The future will offer great opportunities to those with the courage and ability to profit from them. Conversely those who look for a regular, well ordered and secure existence will have good reason to view the next decade with concern and mounting apprehension. The institutional ethos many of us have known in the past is changing beyond recognition. Either we change with it or suffer. Colleges in the future will have less security for their staffs. The demand for courses will be more volatile and the provision more flexible (and probably more temporary). There will be more off-campus activity, with greater emphasis on industrial training in relevant areas.

All this will be reflected in the college library. Will there be organizations within colleges that are still recognizable as libraries? Will they be run by librarians?

We believe that information and materials production centres, highly interactive in their operation, will be at the centre of institutions of further and higher education. They will have to offer a proactive element in student learning *and also* provide an efficient and constantly updated management information system. They will be the responsibility of a team of information 'experts' which will

160

include people with information handling skills. The development of integrated learning resources units is a step in this direction. However it is only a step; the nature and pace of organizational change will become greater from now on. Where librarians fit in these developments may largely depend on circumstances and the individual. Increasingly people will be judged on their ability to deliver rather than a particular set of qualifications. It will be the era of the entrepreneur.

In their early fifties the authors left full-time paid employment. This was a considered decision. Peter Pack is now self-employed offering consultancy and executive services in learning resources. Starting under a government Enterprise Allowance Scheme this has involved him in institutional consultancy; journal editorship; acting as an agency to collect professional advertising; conference planning and organization. Marian voluntarily edits a professional newsletter. We have not retired in the conventional sense. The opportunity existed to perform a creative and developmental role and we took it. In this we find we are by no means alone. Librarians of all ages are moving out of libraries, developing a particular product or skill and marketing it commercially. Examples we have met personally include specialist computer software, information services and interactive video training packages, and there are many more.

The significance of this trend should be obvious to those currently working in the college resource field.

Just as college libraries in the future may not be run by librarians they in turn may take up other types of work. Limited period employment through agencies for young librarians could be one way colleges meet their short-term professional needs. No longer should people think of a single career. Periods of professional work interspersed by education and training for a different type of career will increasingly become the norm.

This then is the exciting, stimulating, unpredictable, uncertain, worrying future facing college librarians. There is no 'end' to this book. In the year 2000 somebody may take the trouble to look back and see how many of our prophesies came true or what developments took place which we had not (and could not have) foreseen. In the meantime . . .

Background reading to Chapters 1 and 2

In Chapters 1 and 2 we are dealing with such a major topic that it has only been possible to treat many of its aspects briefly. Details of works which were used whilst researching the subject are included here for those who wish to pursue the subject in greater depth.

Chapter 1
Business and Technical Education Council, *B/TEC Policies and priorities into the 1990s,* B/TEC, 1984.
'The Business Education Council', *Coombe Lodge Report,* 9, (7), FESC, 1976.
Business Education Council, *First policy statement,* BEC, 1976.
Council for National Academic Awards, *Developments in partnership in validation,* CNAA, 1979.
Council for National Academic Awards, *Future development of the CNAA's academic policies at undergraduate level,* CNAA, 1983.
Council for National Academic Awards, *Quality and validation – future relationships with institutions: a consultative document,* CNAA, 1986.
Council for National Academic Awards, *Response to the government's consultative document on higher education outside the universities,* CNAA, 1982.
Davies, J.L. and Morgan, A.W., *Management of higher education institutions in a period of contraction and uncertainty,* in Boyd-Barrett, O. *et al., Approaches to post-school management: a reader,* Harper & Row, 1983.
Dennison, W.F., *Education in jeopardy: problems and possibilities of contraction,* Blackwell, 1981.
Department of Education and Science, *Future demand for higher education in Great Britain,* Report on education no. 99, HMSO, April 1983.
Department of Education and Science, *The government of colleges of education,* (Chairman Weaver), HMSO, 1966.

Department of Education and Science, *Higher education into the 1990s*, HMSO, 1978.

Department of Education and Science and Local Authority Associations, *Education for the 16-19 year olds*, (Chairman MacFarlane), HMSO, 1980.

Department of Education and Science, National Advisory Council on Education for Industry and Commerce, *Report of the committee on technical courses and examinations*, (Chairman Haslegrave), HMSO, 1969.

Department of Education and Science, *Teacher education and training*, (Chairman James), HMSO, 1972.

Department of Education and Science, Committee of Enquiry into the Academic Validation of Degree Courses in Public Sector Higher Education, *Report, academic validation in public sector higher education*, (Chairman Lindop), Cmnd 9501, HMSO, 1985.

Department of Employment, *Working together: education and training*, HMSO, 1986.

Further Education Curriculum Review and Development Unit, *Loud and clear? Summary of curriculum dissemination in further and higher education*, PR3. FEU, 1980.

'Government policy for the colleges means: "Do more for less"', *NATFHE Journal*, 10, (6), 1985, 23-30.

Hall, V., 'Whatever happened to RVQ?' *NATFHE Journal*, 12, (3), 1987, 20-21

'How to manage when the system goes into reverse', *Coombe Lodge Report*, 15, (4), FESC, 1982.

Jones, D.T.L., *Cost-effectiveness in vocational further education*, Coombe Lodge, Case Study, Information Bank number 1704, FESC, 1981.

'The management of contraction', *Coombe Lodge Report*, 15, (11), FESC, 1983.

Manpower Services Commission and Department of Education and Science, *Review of vocational qualifications in England and Wales*, (Chairman De Ville), interim report, MSC/DES, 1985.

Manpower Services Commission/Local Authority Associations Policy Group, *Work-related NAFE: a guidance handbook*, MSC, 1985.

Moor, C., *et al., TEC Programmes evaluated: student progress and employer perception*, NFER-Nelson, 1983.

National Advisory Council on Education for Industry and Commerce, *The size of classes and approval of further education courses*, NACEIC, 1966.

New, C., 'Is restart a false start?' *NATFHE Journal,* 11, (5), 1986, 16-17.

Peck, D., 'The significance of "competence and competition"', *Education,* 165, (8), 1985, 173.

'Quality in education: do we get what we pay for?', *Coombe Lodge Report,* 15, (5), FESC, 1982.

Technician Education Council, *Policy statement,* TEC, 1974.

Chapter 2

'Assessing educational effectiveness and efficiency', *Coombe Lodge Report,* 18, (3), FESC, 1985.

Birch, D.W., *FEMIS and the SSR,* Coombe Lodge FEMIS Working Paper, Information Bank Number 1697, FESC, 1984.

Birch, D.W. and Latcham, J., 'The Audit Commission and FE: value for money and the audit ratios', *Coombe Lodge Report,* 18, (3), 1985.

Birch, D.W. and Latcham, J., 'The Audit Commission and FE', *Education,* 166, (12), 1985, 264.

Birch, D.W. and Latcham, J., 'Where the Audit Commission failed to take its own advice', *Education,* 166, (13), 1985, 287.

Burton, H. and Mauger, S., 'The Open College and its support service requirements', *Learning Resources Journal,* 3, (2), 56-65.

'Capping the pool', *Coombe Lodge Report,* 13, (4), FESC, 1980.

Chartered Institute of Public Finance and Accountancy, *Measuring efficiency in the public sector,* CIPFA, 1982.

Cuthbert, R.E., 'FEMIS: how the system works', *NATFHE Journal,* 9, (8), 1984, 13.

Cuthbert, R.E., *The management of further education and the further education management information system (FEMIS),* Coombe Lodge, FEMIS Paper, Information Bank Number 1978, FESC, 1984.

'Dicing with HE: the NAB/DES tug of war', *NATFHE Journal,* 11, (2) 1986, 19-22.

Jones, J. and Liggett, K., 'FEMIS: a management tool with a cutting edge', *NATFHE Journal,* 9, (8), 1984, 28-30.

The SRHE Leverhulme series

i   Lindley, R. *(ed.), Higher education and the labour market,* SRHE monograph 43, 1981.

ii   Fulton, O. (ed.), *Access to higher education,* SRHE monograph 44, 1981.

iii   Wagner, L. (ed.), *Agenda for institutional change in higher education,* SRHE monograph 45, 1982.

iv   Oldham, G. (ed.), *The future of research,* SRHE monograph 47, 1982.

v   Robinson, K. (ed.), *The arts and higher education,* SRHE monograph 48, 1982.

vi   Bligh, D. (ed.), *Professionalism and flexibility for learning,* SRHE monograph 49, 1982.

vii Bligh, D. (ed.), *Accountability or freedom for teachers?* SRHE monograph 50, 1982.

viii Morris, A. and Sizer, J. (eds), *Resources and higher education,* SRHE monograph 51, 1983.

ix   Shattock, M. (ed.), *The structure and governance of higher education,* SRHE monograph 52, 1983.

x   Williams, G. and Blackstone, T. (eds), *Response to adversity: higher education in a harsh climate,* SRHE monograph 53, 1983.

Summers, J., 'Open college – open questions', *NATFHE Journal,* 12, (3), 1987, 16-17.

Appendix: Acronyms used in the text

AALS   Association of American Library Schools
ACUCHE   Association of Computer Units in Colleges of Higher
            Education
AFE   Advanced Further Education
AIMER   Access to Information on Multicultural Educational
            Resources
AMA   Association of Municipal Authorities
ASLIB   Association of Special Libraries and Information
            Bureaux
ATS   Adult Training Scheme
BARD   British Database on Research into Aids for the
            Disabled
BEC   Business Education Council
BLAISE   British Library Automated Information Service
BTEC   Business and Technical Education Council
CAL   Computer Assisted Learning
CATE   Council for Accreditation of Teacher Education
CBI   Confederation of British Industries
CCETSWA   Central Council for Education and Training in Social
            Work
CD/ROM   Compact Disc/Read Only Memory
CIPFA   Chartered Institute of Public Finance and Account-
            ancy
CLEA   Council of Local Education Authorities
CNAA   Council for National Academic Awards
COM   Computer Output Microfilm
CPD   Continuing Professional Development
CPVE   Certificate of Pre-vocational Education
DES   Department of Education and Science
DOE   Department of Employment
DTI   Department of Trade and Industry
ECCTIS   Educational Counselling and Credit Transfer Infor-
            mation Service

EMIE	Educational Management Information Exchange
ERIC	Educational Resources Information Center
ESA	Employment Services Agency
FE	Further Education
FEMIS	Further Education Management Information System
FERN	Further Education Research Network
FESC	Further Education Staff College
FEU	Further Education (Curriculum Review and Development) Unit
HE	Higher Education
HMI	Her Majesty's Inspector
HOD	Head of Department
IT	Information Technology
ITAP	Information Technology Advisory Panel
JTS	Job Training Scheme
LA	Library Association
LAA	Local Authorities Association
LACOFHE	Library Association Colleges of Further and Higher Education Section
LEA	Local Education Authority
LR	Learning Resources
LRDG	Learning Resources Deveopment Group
MARIS	Materials and Resources Information Service
MEDLARS	Medical Literature Analysis and Retrieval System
MSC	Manpower Services Commission
NAB	National Advisory Body (on Local Authority Higher Education)
NAFE	Non-Advanced Further Education
NATFHE	National Association of Teachers in Further and Higher Education
NCET	National Council for Educational Technology
NCVQ	National Council for Vocational Qualifications
NEDO	National Economic Development Office
NERIS	National Educational Information Resources Service
NUS	National Union of Students
PCFC	Polytechnic Central Funding Council
RAC	Regional Advisory Councils
RSA	Royal Society for the Encouragement of Arts, Manufactures and Commerce
RVQ	Review of Vocational Qualifications

SRHE	Society for Research into Higher Education
SSR	Staff Student Ratios
STEP	Special Temporary Employment Programme
TEC	Technical Education Council
TES	Times Educational Supplement
TSA	Training Services Agency
TTNS	The Times Network Service
TUC	Trades Union Congress
TVEI	Technical Vocational Education Initiative
UGC	University Grants Committee
UVP	Unified Vocational Preparation
WEEP	Work Experience Programme
WOW	World of Work
WRNAFE	Work Related Non Advanced Further Education
YOP	Youth Opportunities Programme
YTS	Youth Training Scheme

Index

Note The 'All through' method of alphabetization is used. Terms consisting solely of initials are placed at the front of each alphabetical letter sequence.

171

resources unit: ethos 61, 78ff., 91,
135, 137, 148
course: college librarian's role 65
expansion in education *see* higher and
further education: expansion factors
expert systems *see* computing: fifth
generation

FEMIS *see* Further Education
Management Information System
FERN *see* Further Education Research
Network
FESC *see* Further Education Staff
College
FEU *see* Further Education Unit
feedback *see* evaluation
fifth generation computing *see*
computing: fifth generation
flexibility
college library management 61
education patterns *see* learning
patterns
flexistudy: Barnet College 74
floor plans: college library *see* college
library: floor plans
funding
colleges 6, 8, 12, 20, 53, 73, 77
college library 67, 155
students 25
further education *see also* higher and
further education; non-advanced
further education
Further Education Management
Information System 8, 22
further education: public sector:
historical review 3
Further Education Research Network
108
Further Education Staff College 10, 81,
157
Further Education Unit 10, 23, 74
databases 108
futurology: college library 159–61

GNP *see* gross national product
gateways *see* databases: access: gateways
'Getting Started' package: interactive
video 115
goal conflict 79
goal displacement 65

'Good Management Practice' report 21
government policies: education 12
Grolier Videodisc Encyclopaedia of
Science and Technology 113
gross national product: education
percentage 4
guiding: college library *see* college
library: guiding

HMI *see* Her Majesty's Inspectors
Head of LR
consultancy: value *see* consultancy:
value: Head of LR
place in college management structure
see college management structure:
place of Head of LR
promotion from college librarian *see*
college librarian: promotion to
Head of LR
Her Majesty's Inspectors: visits to
colleges 69
higher and further education
contraction factors 5
expansion factors 5
higher education *see also* further
education
'Higher Education; Meeting the
Challenge' (Cm 114) *see* Command
Paper 114
higher education: public sector: historical
review 3
Holland Report 10
human resources *see* resources: human
hybrid posts 153

ITAP *see* Information Technology
Advisory Panel
image: college library 94
independent learning *see* learning:
independent
independent learning centres 145
independent study programmes *see*
learning: independent study
programmes
individualized learning *see* learning:
individualized
industrial liaison officer 67
industry: college relationship with 12
Industry Year 7
information handling skills 61, 104

176